Introduction

I'm a mixed-media and collage artist and enjoy making art with many different mediums. I love animals, most especially dogs and cats, so a lot of my art features these endearing creatures, which is why many of the images I produce using A.I. focus on nature and animals. These a couple of my "real" paintings.

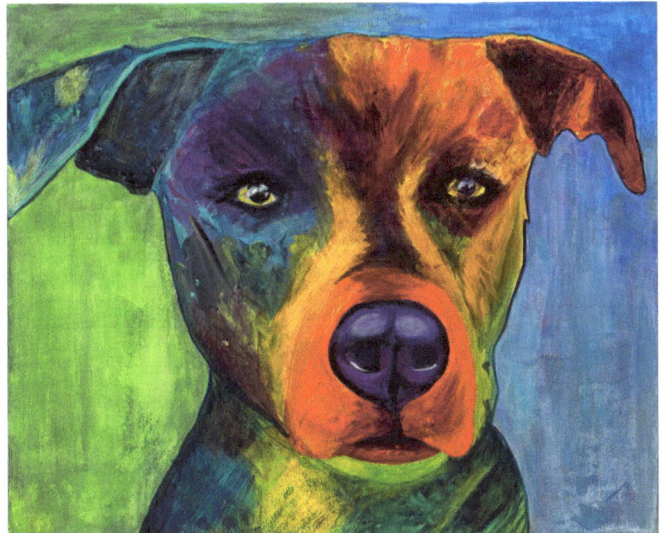

Moosh - acrylic on canvas

Melancholy Baby - oil sticks on canvas

Since discovering the fun of creating images with artificial intelligence I have completely fallen in love with it, to the extent that it might be called an addiction! I am constantly amazed by the incredible art produced by this technology. Sadly, there is a lot of fear and negativity surrounding A.I. but it is really just another tool for creativity.

In the unfolding tapestry of the digital era, the intersection of art and technology is vibrant, intricate, and constantly evolving. Gone are the days when brushes, chisels, and canvases were the sole instruments of an artist. Today, algorithms, codes, and digital platforms have joined the ensemble, introducing a symphony of possibilities. Across centuries, art has undergone countless transformations, shaped by the tools and visions of its time. In our present chapter, artificial intelligence stands as a new collaborator, amplifying human creativity and pushing the boundaries of what's imaginable. Rather than supplanting human touch, A.I. acts as a conduit, expanding our artistic lexicon and introducing dimensions hitherto unexplored.

The Midjourney app, in my opinion, stands at the forefront of this revolution, enabling artists and enthusiasts alike to merge their intrinsic creativity with the prowess of artificial intelligence. A beacon for both seasoned artists and novices, Midjourney provides a platform to harness the power of A.I. to inspire creativity and craft unique art. The advent of A.I. in art isn't a replacement for human creativity; instead, it's an augmentation, opening doors to uncharted realms of imagination.

I hope these pictures and prompts open your eyes to the amazing opportunities in A.I. This book is purely just a book of prompts with the corresponding images that were made with them. Using the exact same prompt is unlikely to produce an identical image, but it will be a close variation, and a good starting point for you to create your own. If you have not yet experimented with Midjourney, there are many places to learn about it, most notably https://docs.midjourney.com, and also YouTube has many videos showing how to get started.

Sam

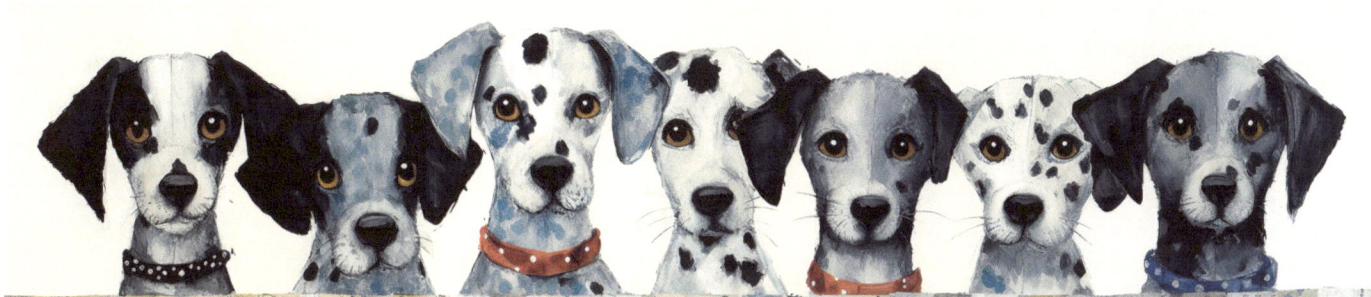

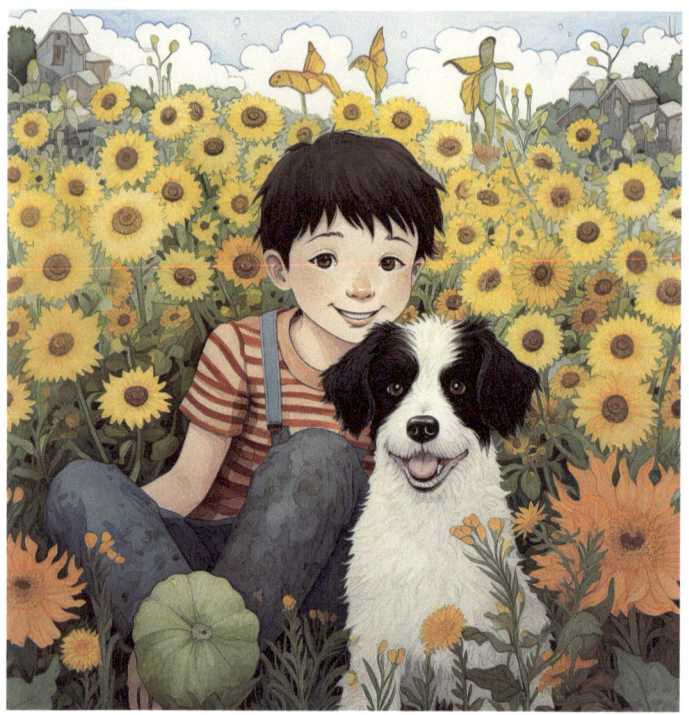

the cover of a children's book showing a boy and his dog, in the style of lucy grossmith, junji ito, cheerful colors --v 5.2

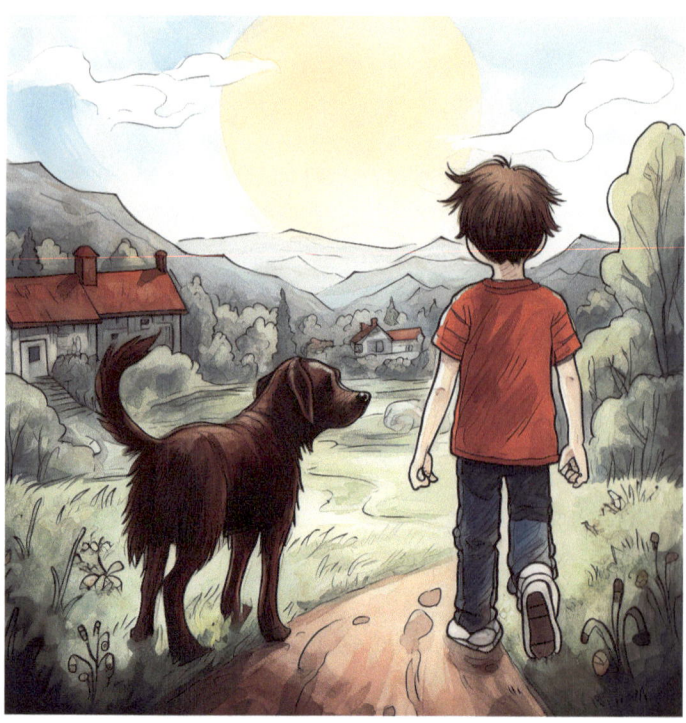

the boy and dog by carl p symonson, in the style of colorful drawings, english countryside, cute and dreamy --v 5.2

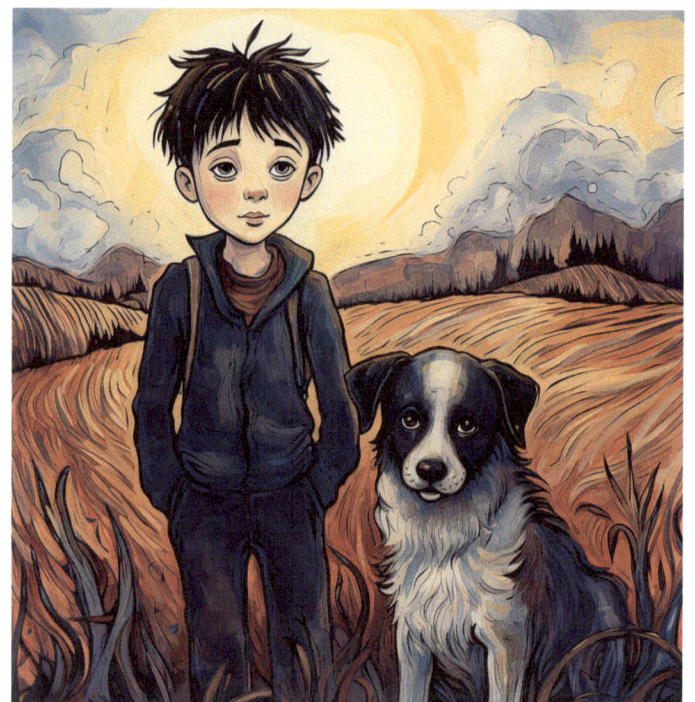

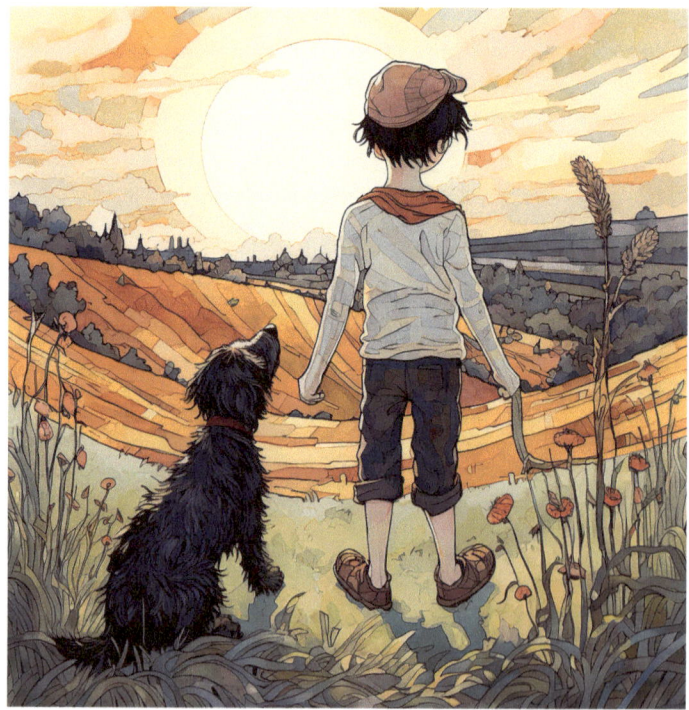

the boy and the dog by shirley mcleod, in the style of dreamlike illustration, colorful drawings, english countryside, youthful protagonists, ultrafine detail, wandering eye --v 5.2

painted watercolor illustration of a bichon frise sitting on the sidewalk, in the style of Venetian scenes --v 5.2 --ar 4:5 --s 250

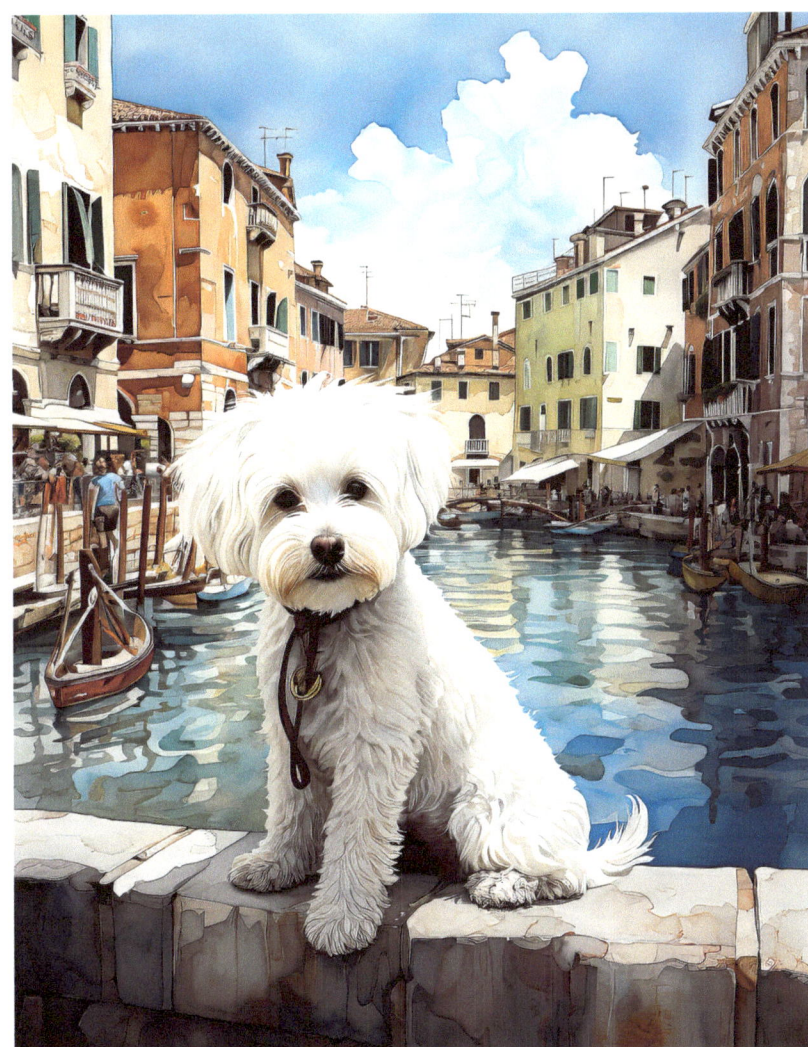

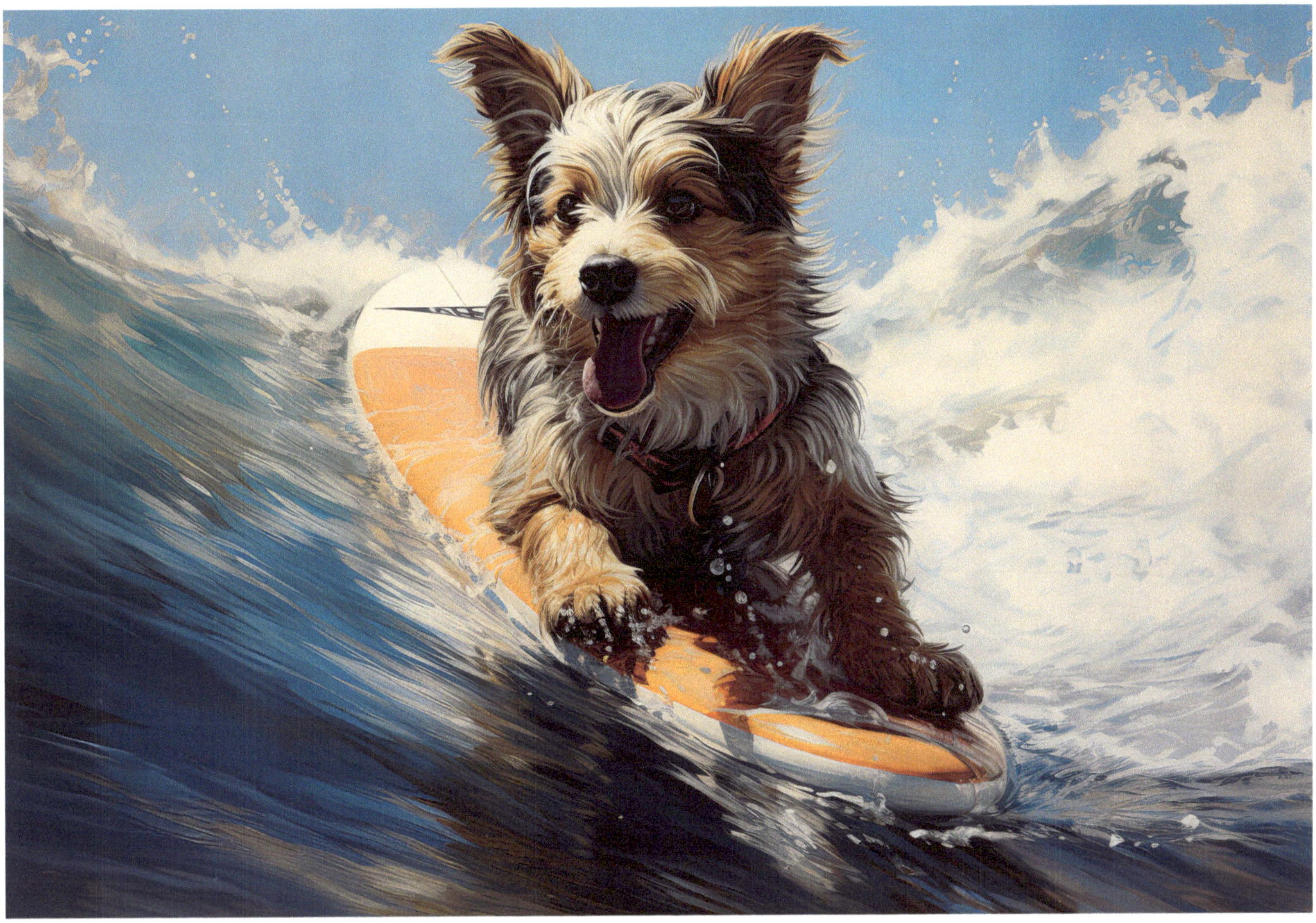

whimsical painting of a dog on the surfboard, in the style of vivid realism, high resolution --ar 3:2 --v 5.2 --s 250

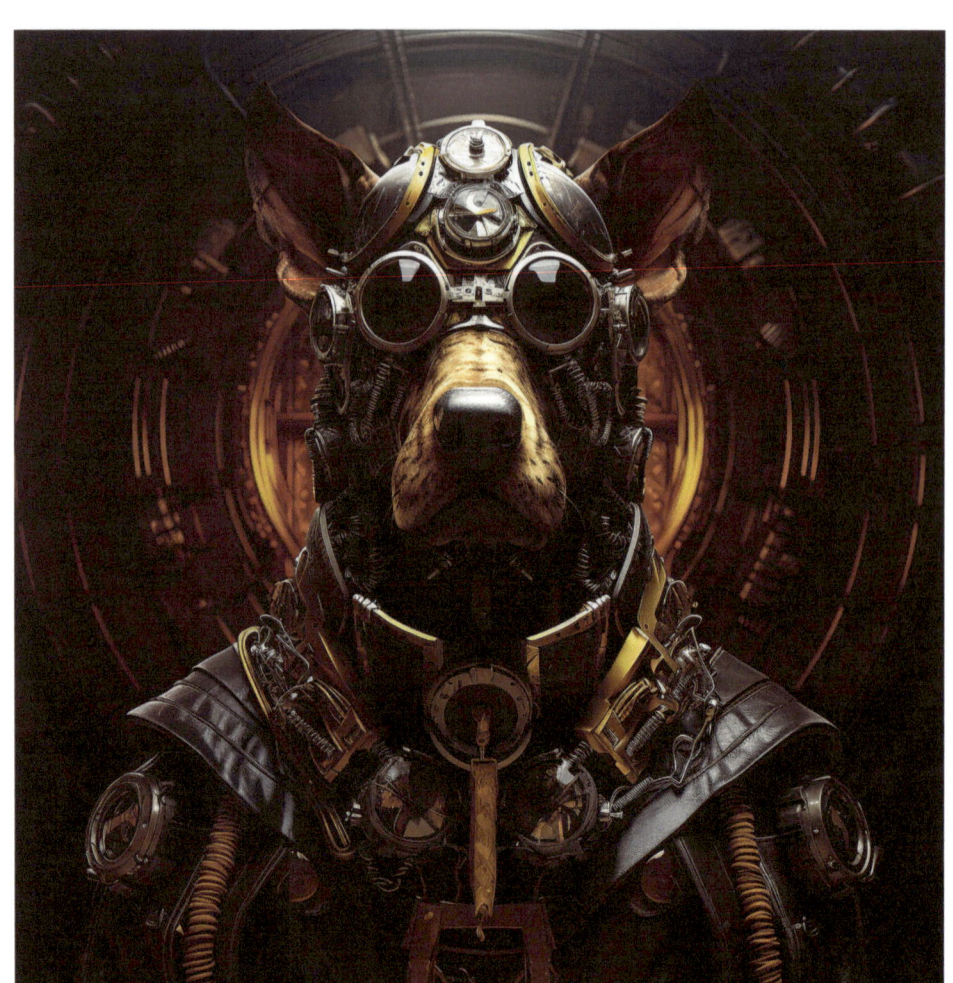

steampunk dog steampunk image, in the style of futuristic realism, hieratic visionary, grandiose portraits, redshift, contemporary take on medieval art, geometric animal figures, kingcore --v 5.2 --s 250

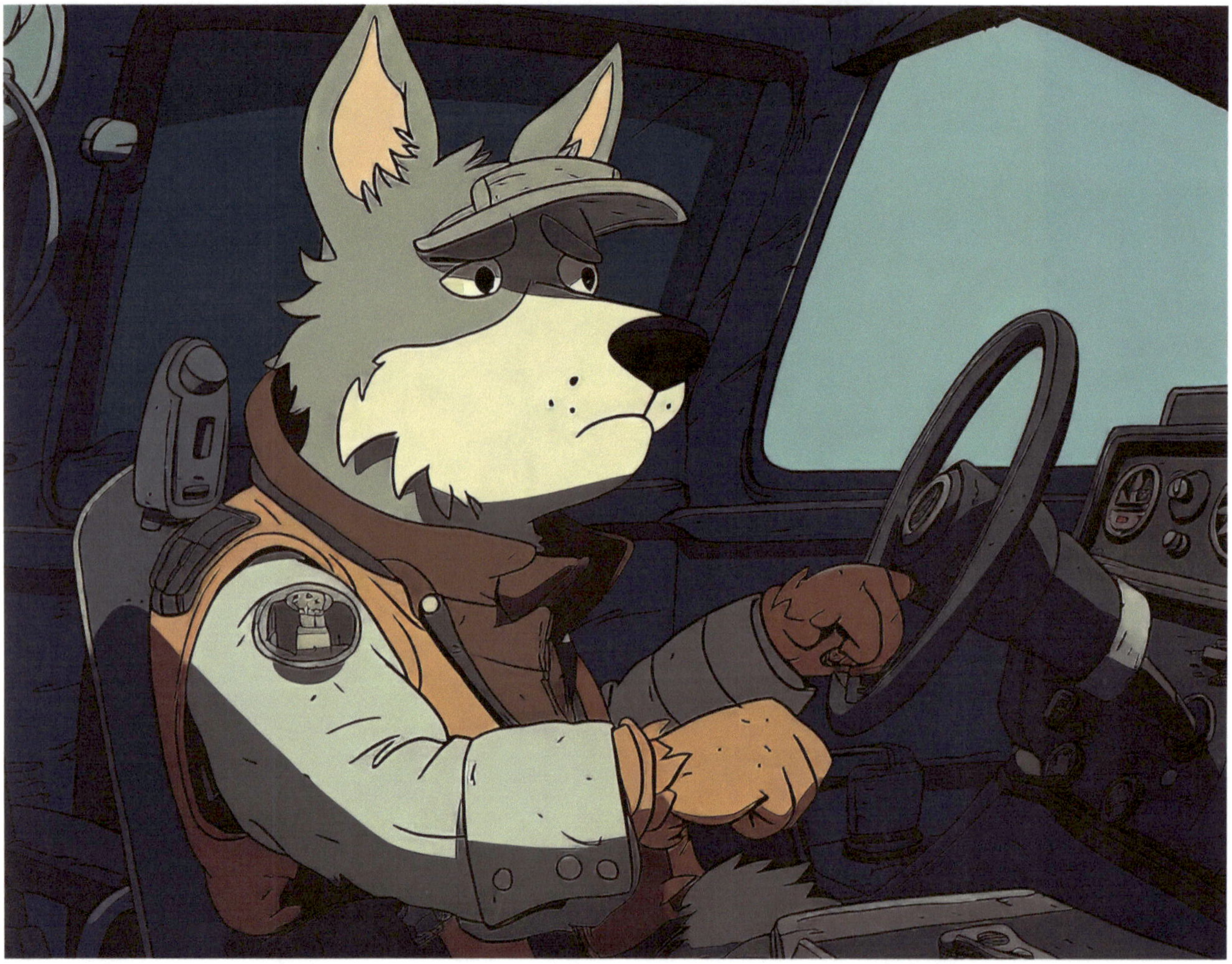

an adult dog sitting behind the steering wheel of a car, in the style of toonami, humorous animal scenes --ar 4:3 --s 250 --v 5

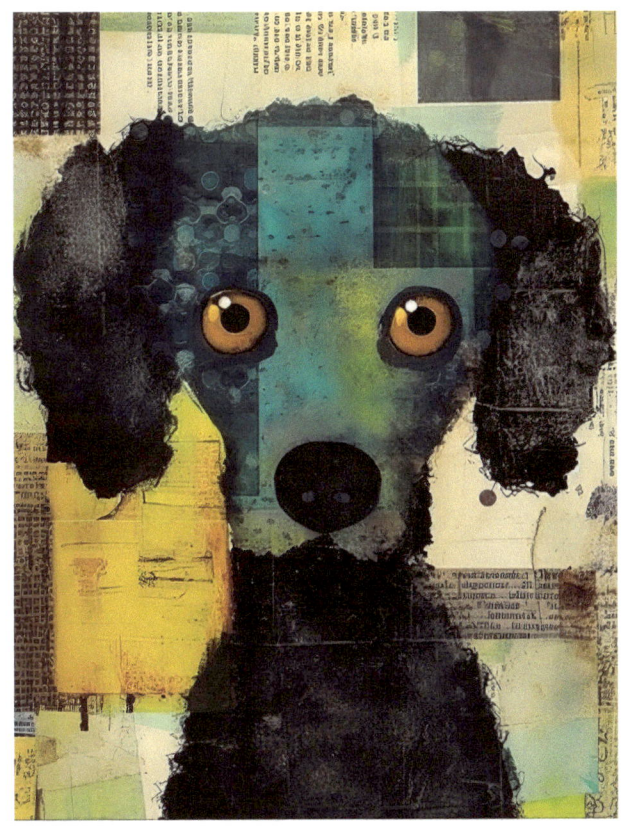

a painting of a dog laying on a bed, in the style of fauvism precursor, color field paintings, sleepycore, terracotta, zaire school of popular painting, en plein air beach scenes --v 5.2 --ar 3:2

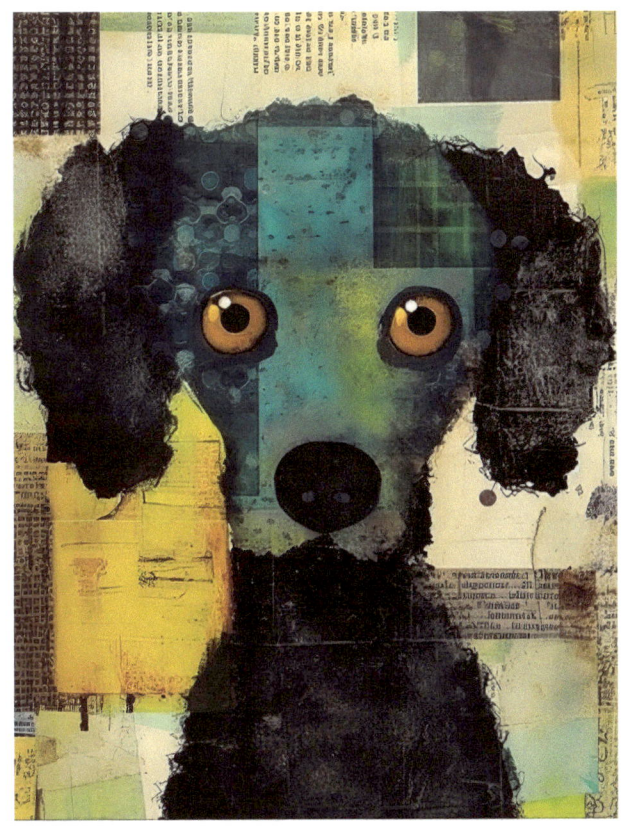
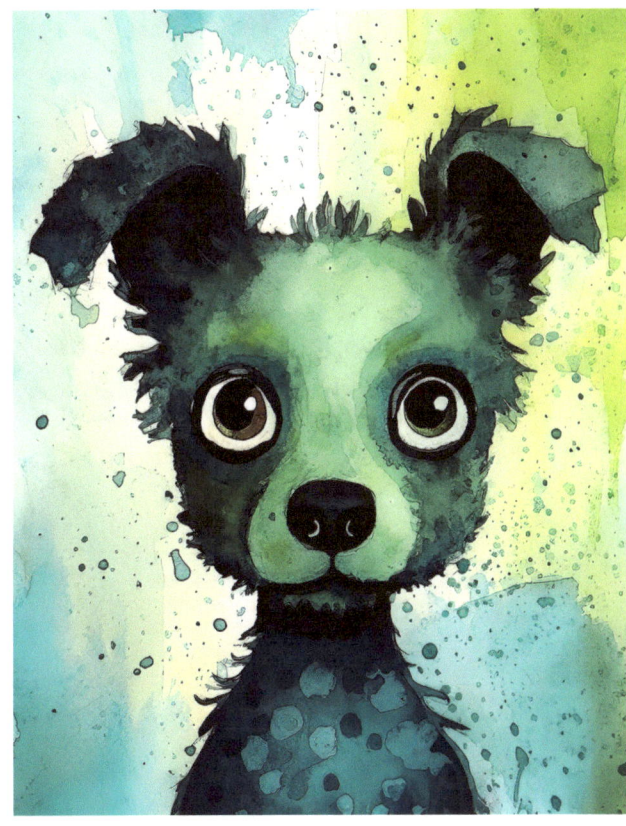

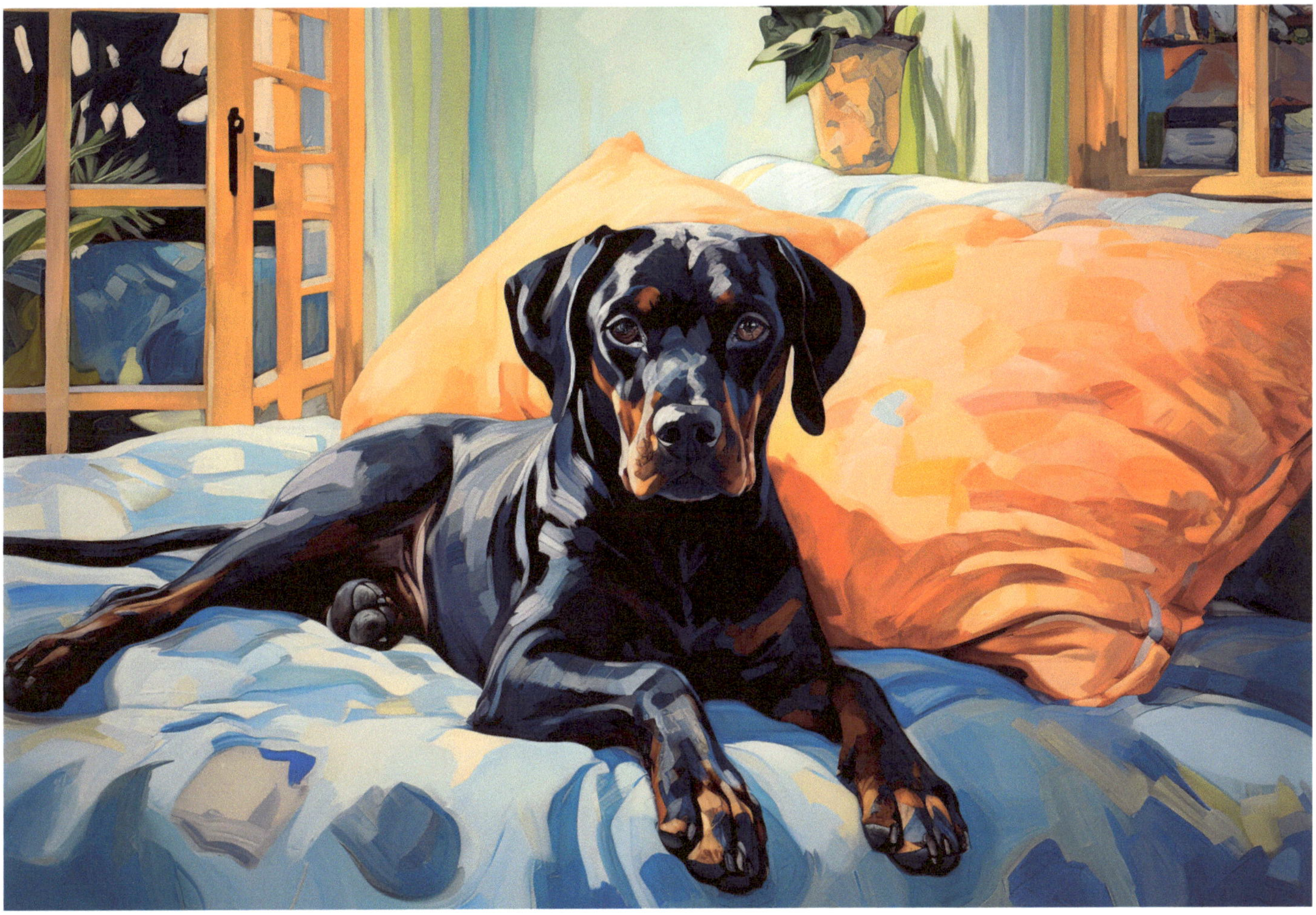

a painting of a dog with green eyes, in the style of mid-century illustration, poodlepunk, yellow and dark blue, stains/washes --v 5.2 --ar 85:110 --s 250 --style raw

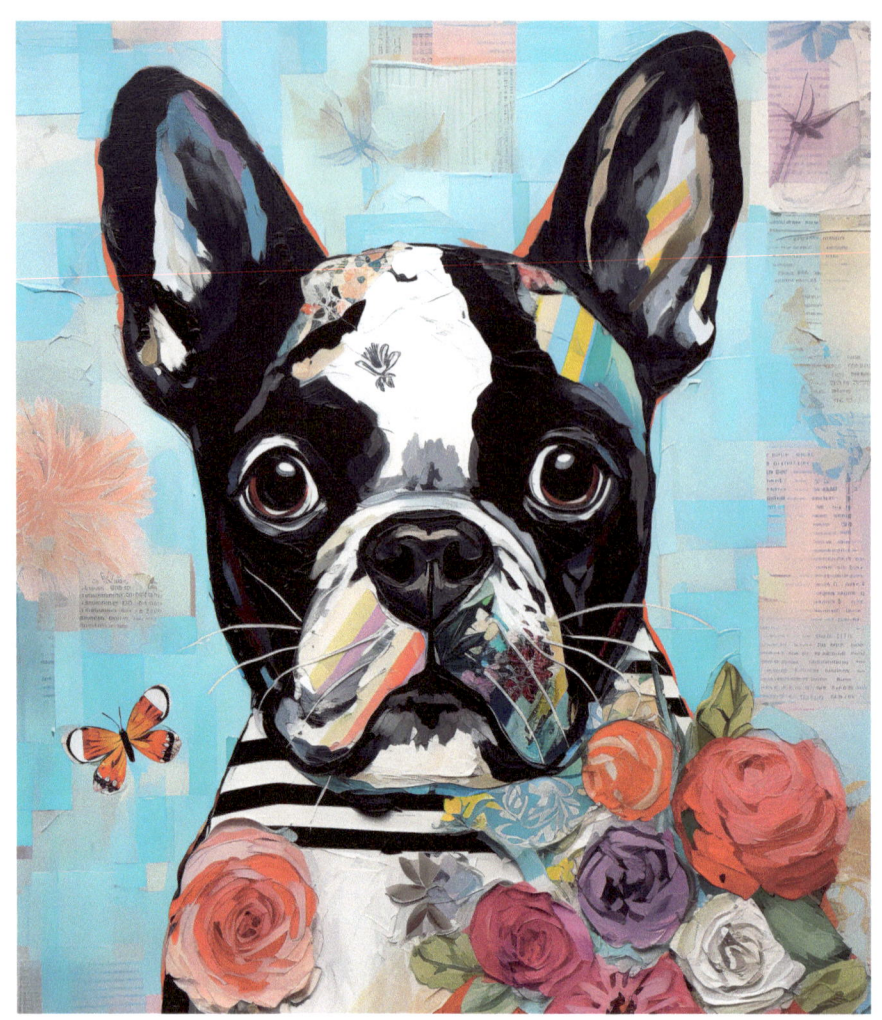

cute quirky french bulldog puppy with flowers art, in the style of playful lines, teal and black, a collage of mixed media art made with tissue paper, magazine and newspaper clippings, oil paint, graphite pencil lines and fabric, in the style of playful surrealism, whimsical --ar 85:110 --v 5.2 --style raw

an image of a n american bulldog dog in a newspaper, in the style of textural elements and collages, layers of paint, recycled material murals,nonrepresentational, portrait --ar 4:5 --s 250 --v 5.1

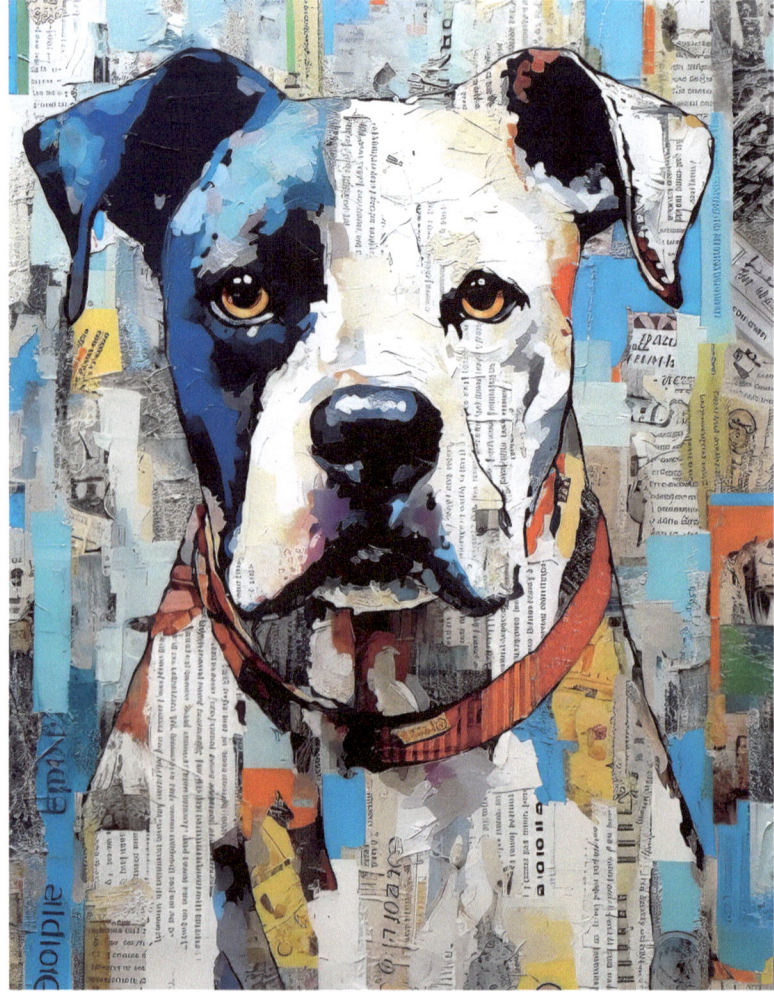

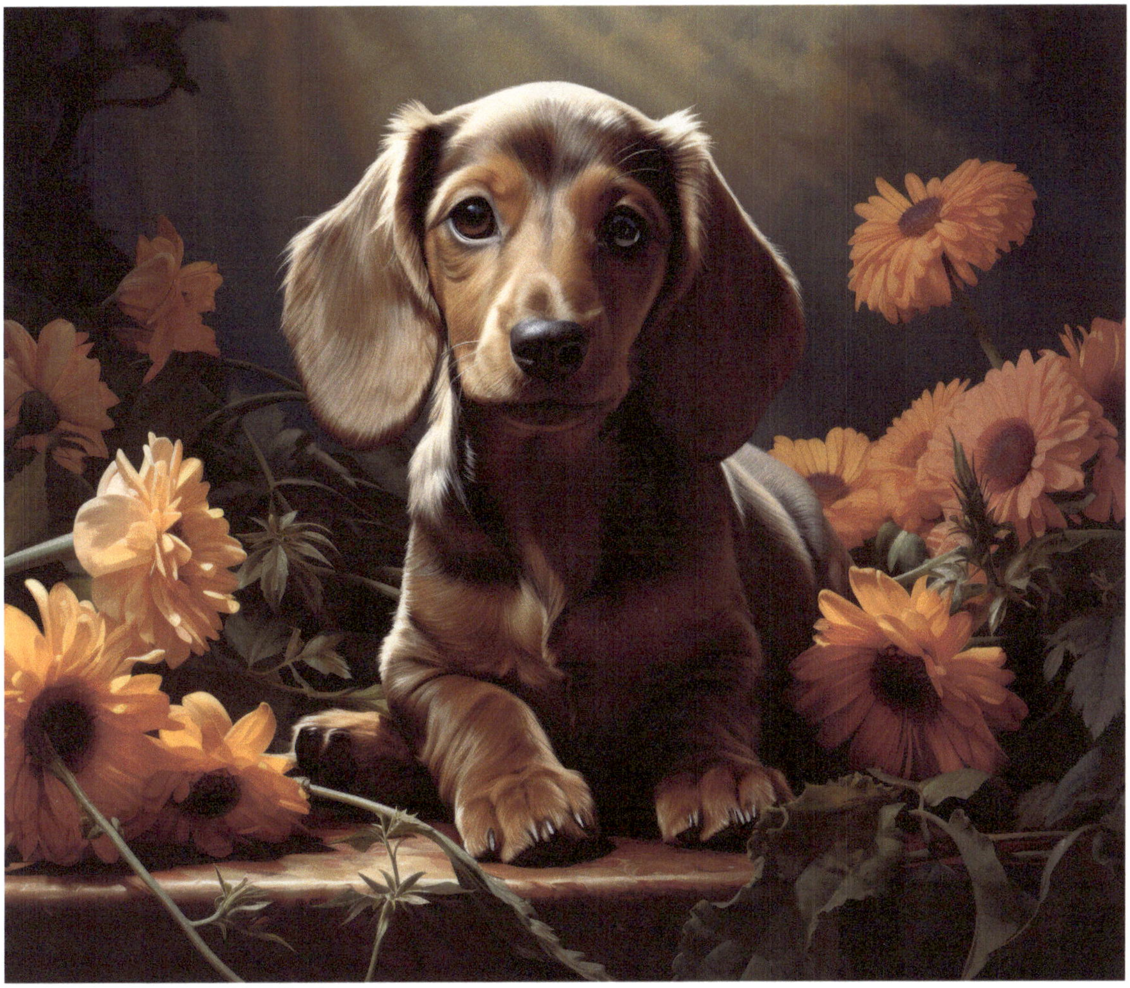

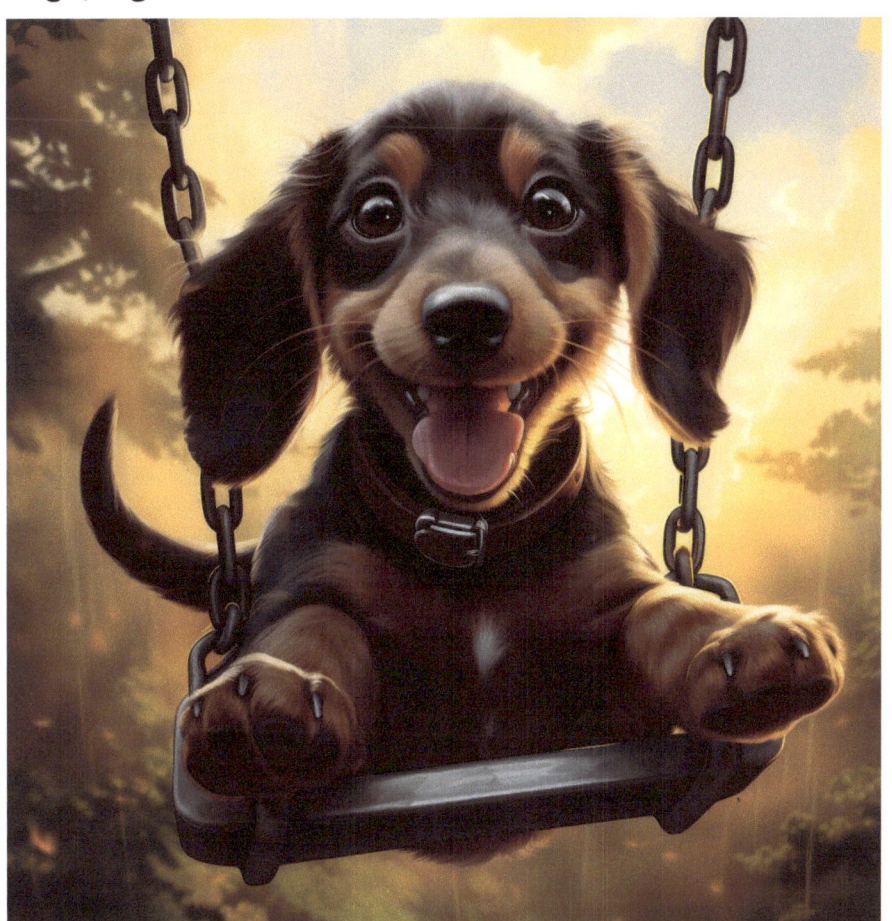

dachshund i love you so in the style of realistic and hyper-detailed renderings, digital illustration --ar 32:27 --v 5.2 --s 250

dachshund swing happy love the breed, in the style of digital airbrushing, cartoony --v 5.2 --s 250

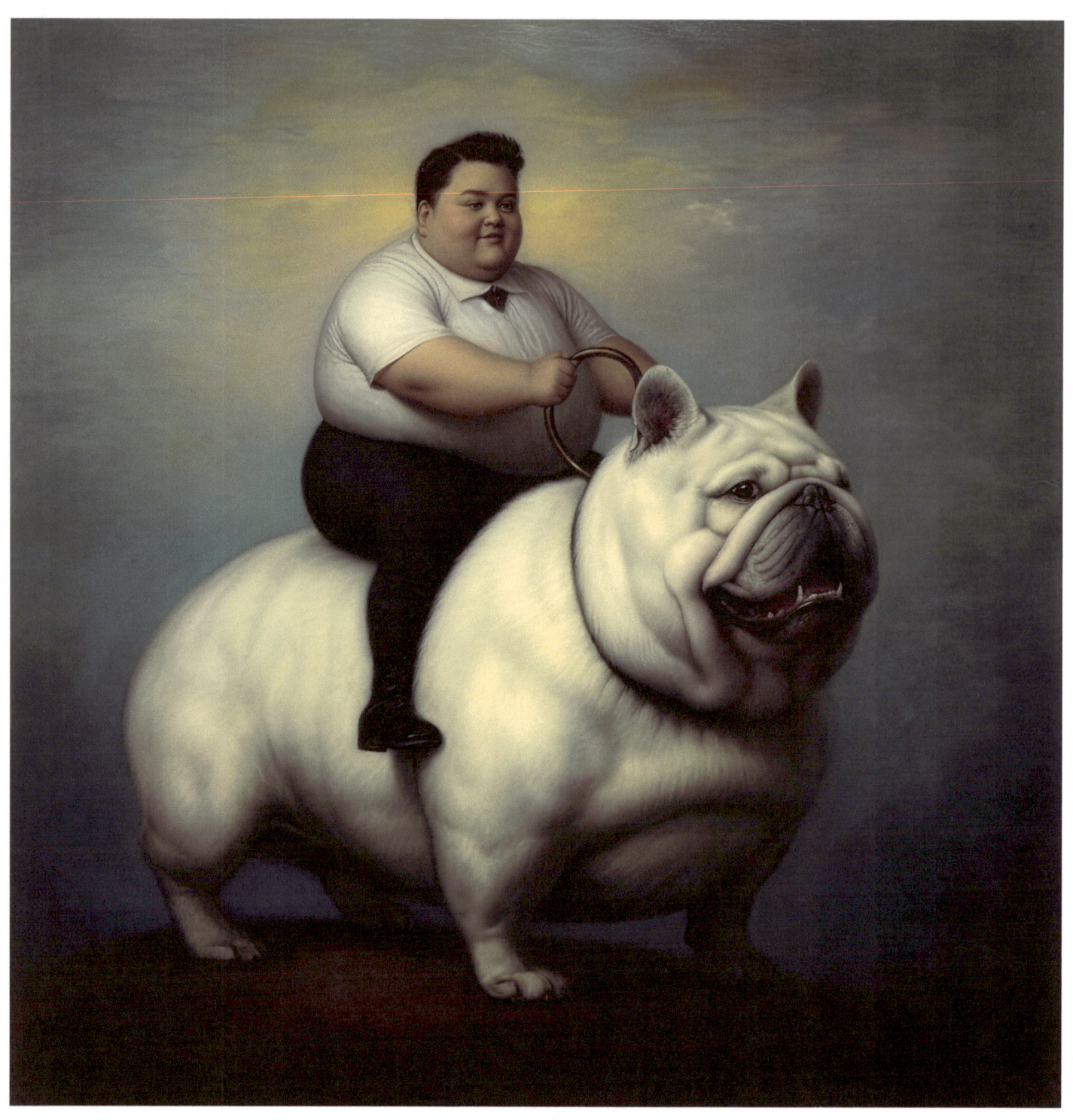

fat baby riding on a fat dog --v 5.1 --s 750

little girl with a dog for bewildering dolls, in the style of neo-pop surrealism, mandy disher, mark ryden, large canvas paintings, serene faces, dark white and pink, child-like innocence --v 5.2 --s 250

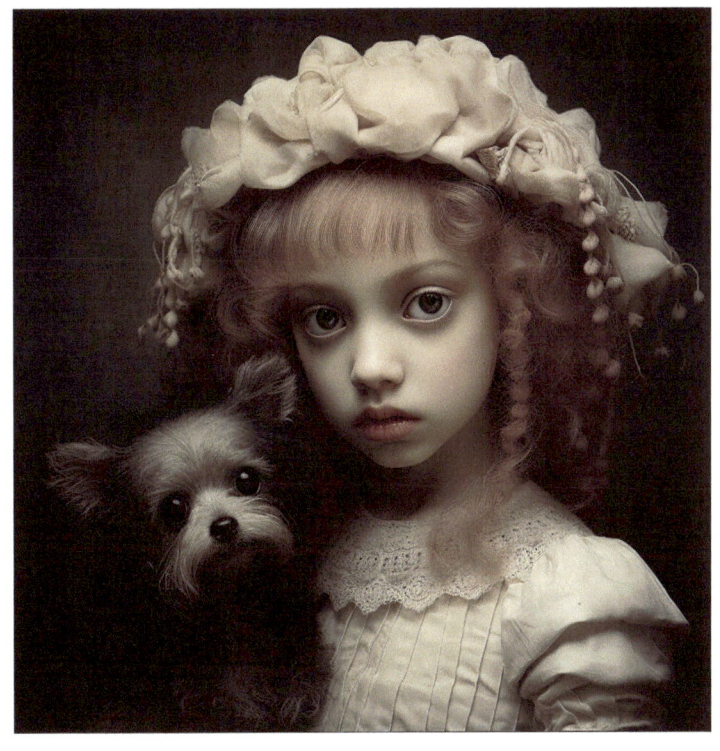

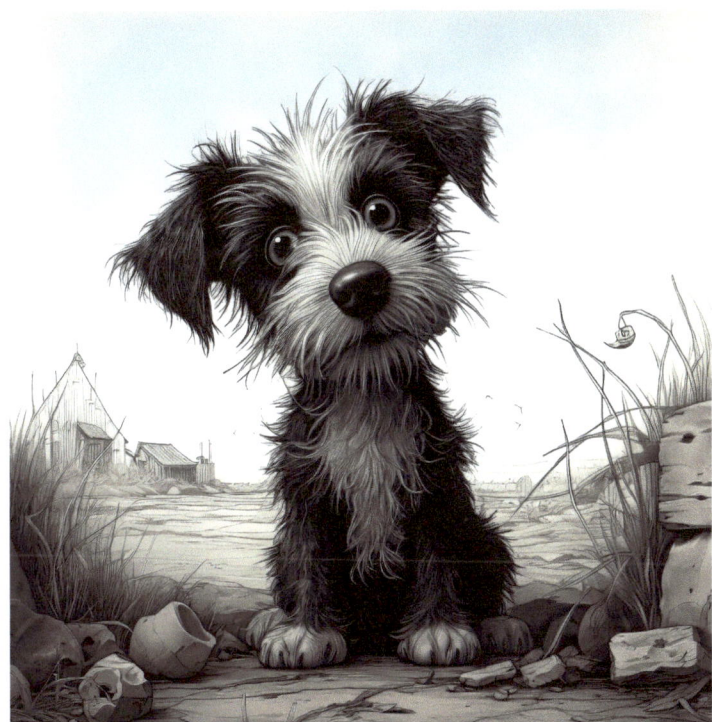

a cute little cartoon dog with short hair, in the style of whimsical realism, flickr, detailed crosshatching, sonian, whimsical children's book illustrator, disney animation, spiky mounds --v 5.2 --s 250

good morning brown pomeranian pixar style, 2D illustration, illustration style, very cute, picture book --v 5.2 --s 250

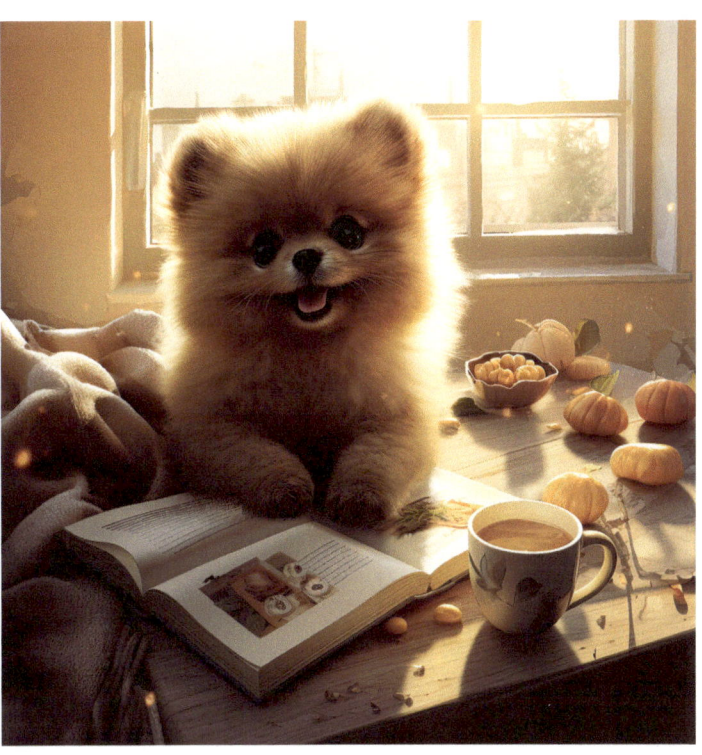

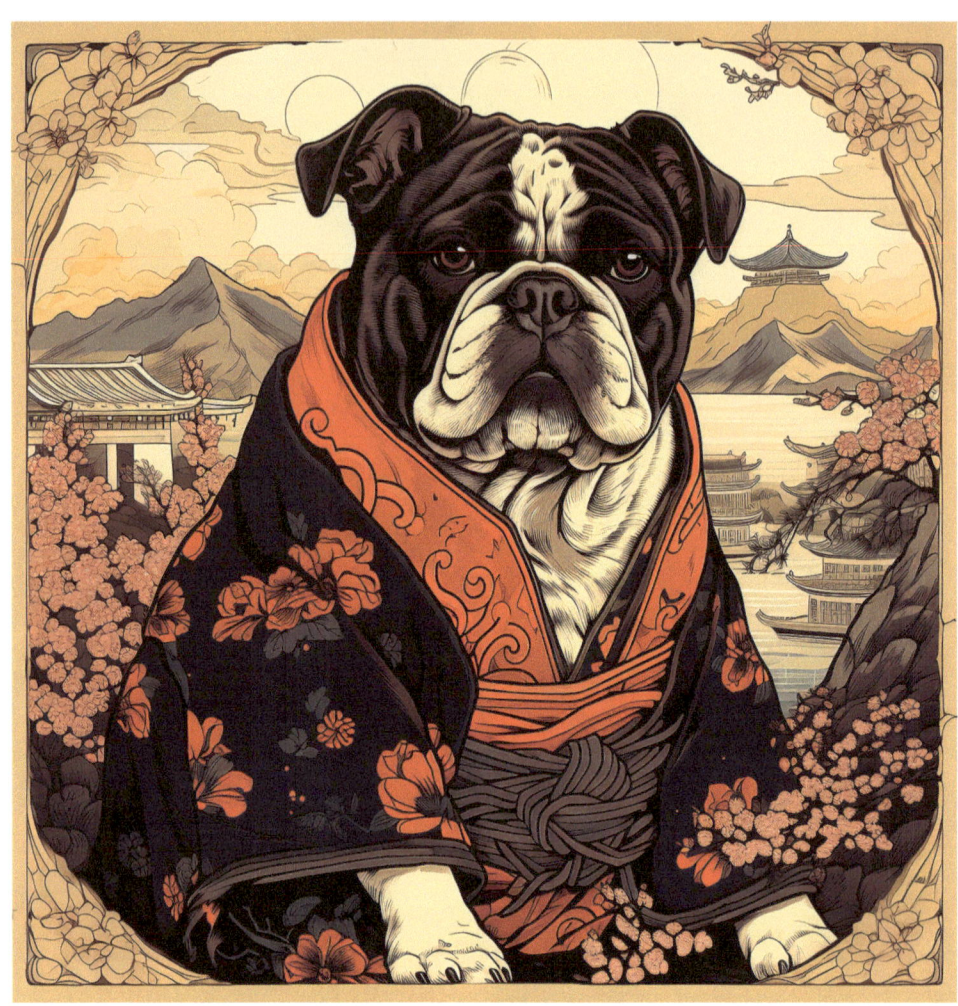

Cute dogs with fat faces in Ukiyo-e style --v 5.2 --s 250

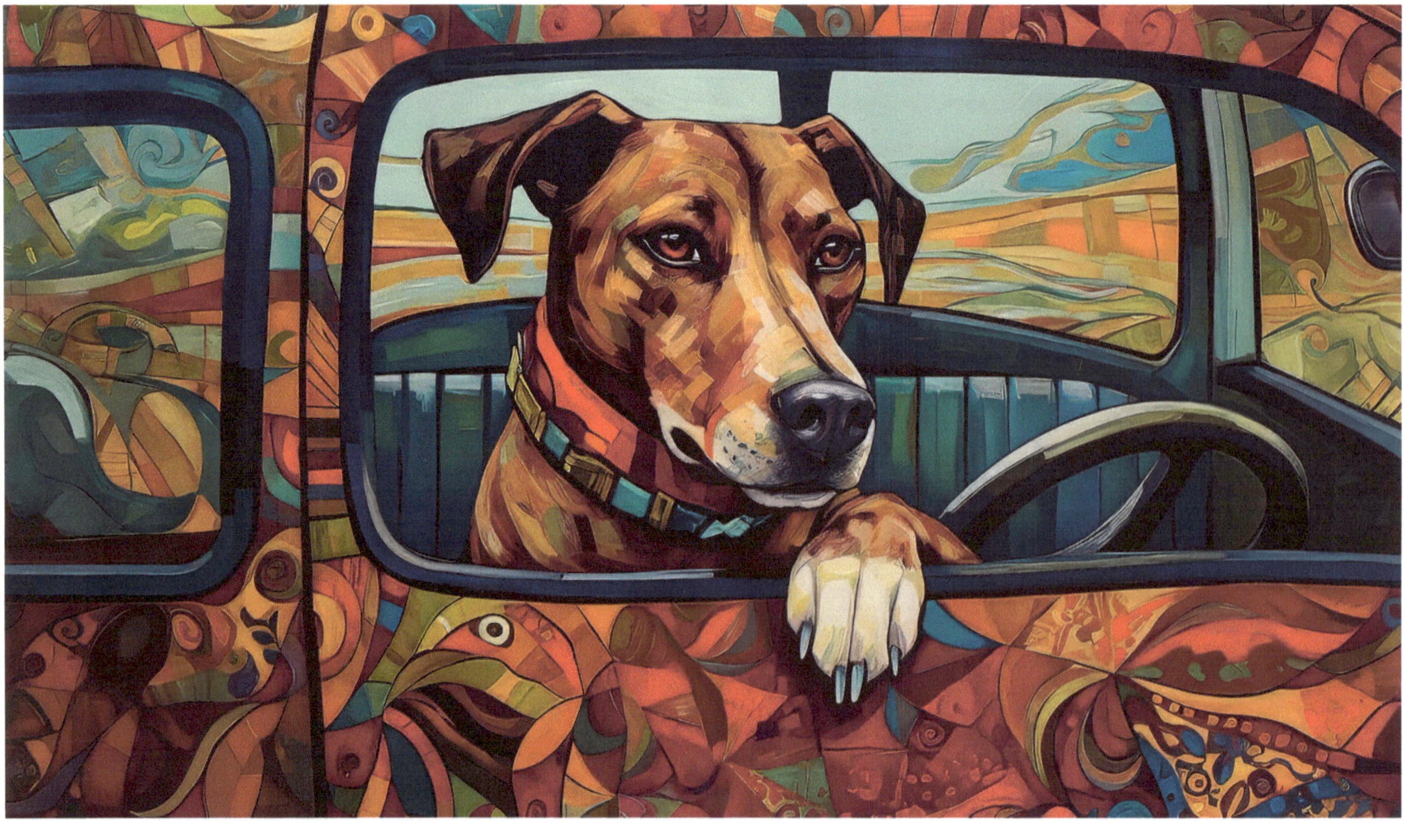

a dog driving the car, uhd image, naive, wlad safronow, southern countryside, dignified poses, tondo --ar 16:9 --s 250 --v 5

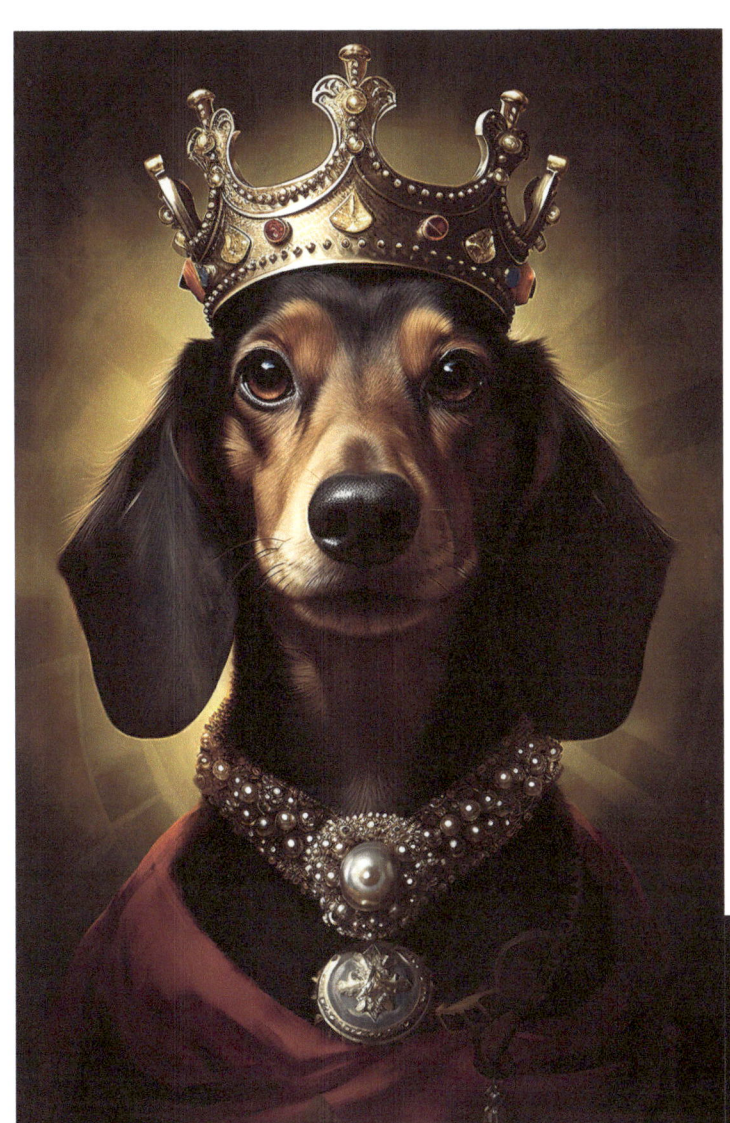

the king dachshund dog by thomas macleod, in the style of digital painting, gothic grandeur, elegant realism, detailed costumes, charming characters, classical elegance, petcore --v 5.2 --ar 75:112

the queen poodle dog by thomas macleod, in the style of digital painting, gothic grandeur, elegant realism, detailed costumes, charming characters, classical elegance, petcore --v 5.2 --ar 75:112

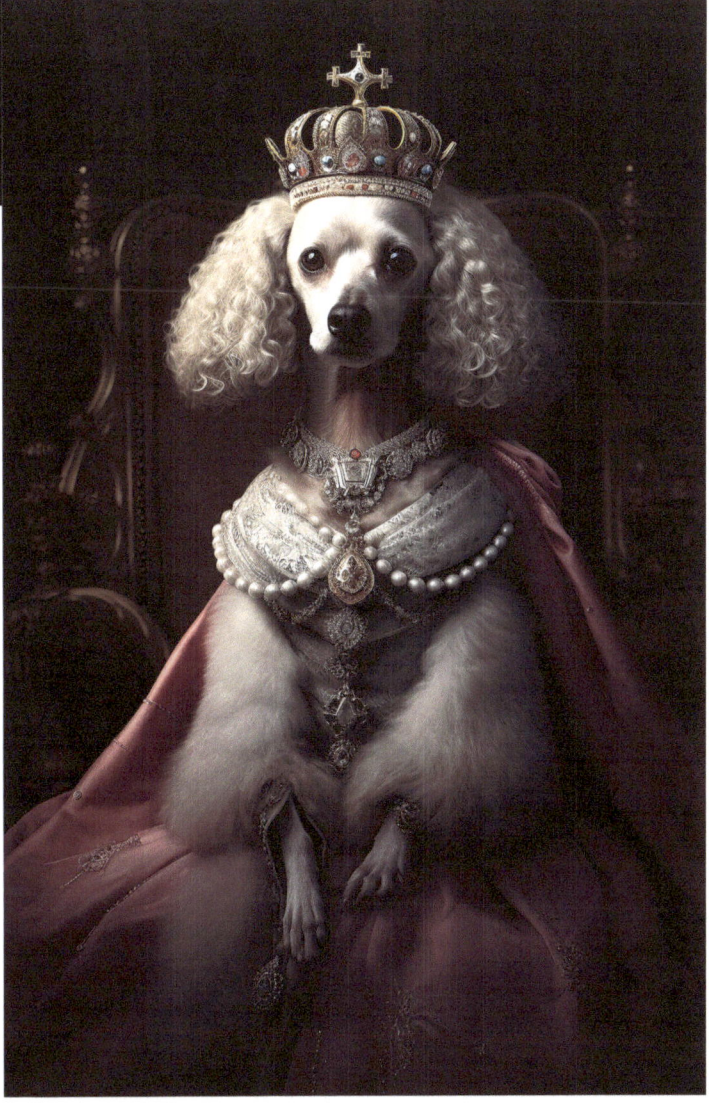

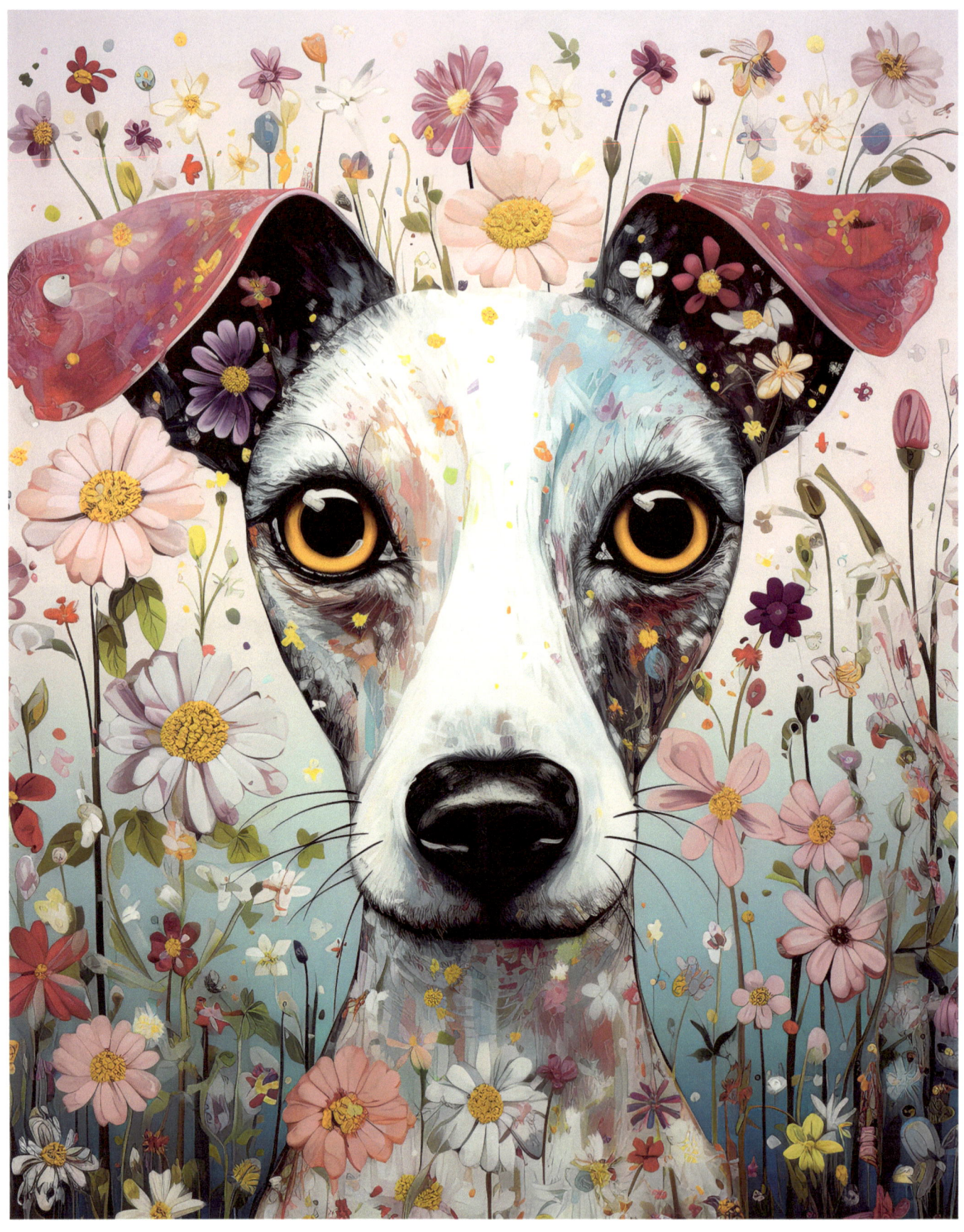

a dog with flowers in its eyes painted on canvas, in the style of jane crowther, light white and light magenta, toyen, lithograph, steve henderson, multilayered dimensions --v 5.2 --ar 25:31

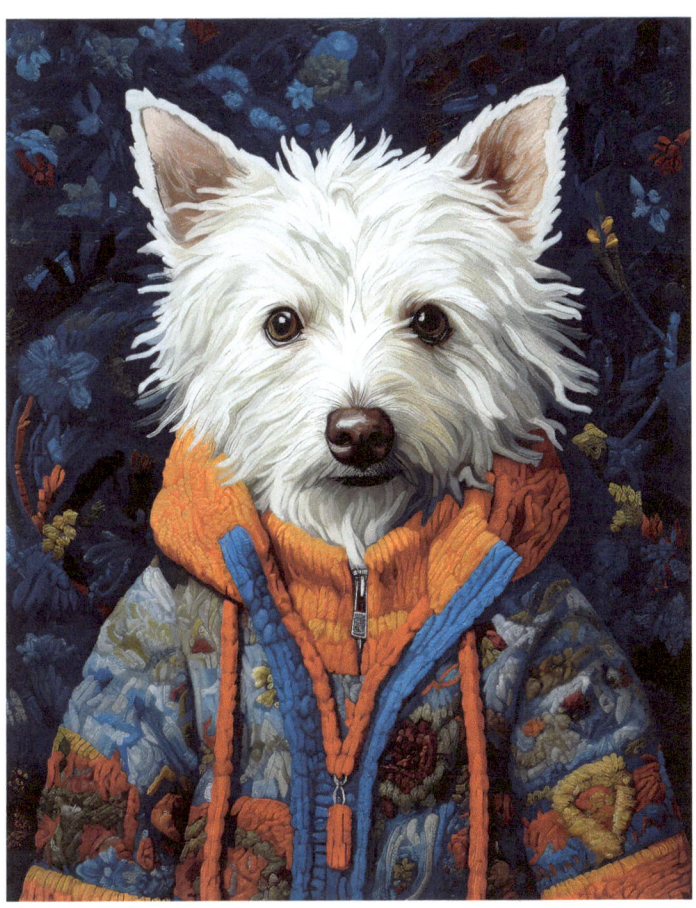

an oil painting of a white dog wearing a blue sweater, in the style of folk art inspired, fiber art, elaborate beadwork, light indigo and orange, dolly kei, precisionist art
--v 5.2 --ar 4:5 --s 250

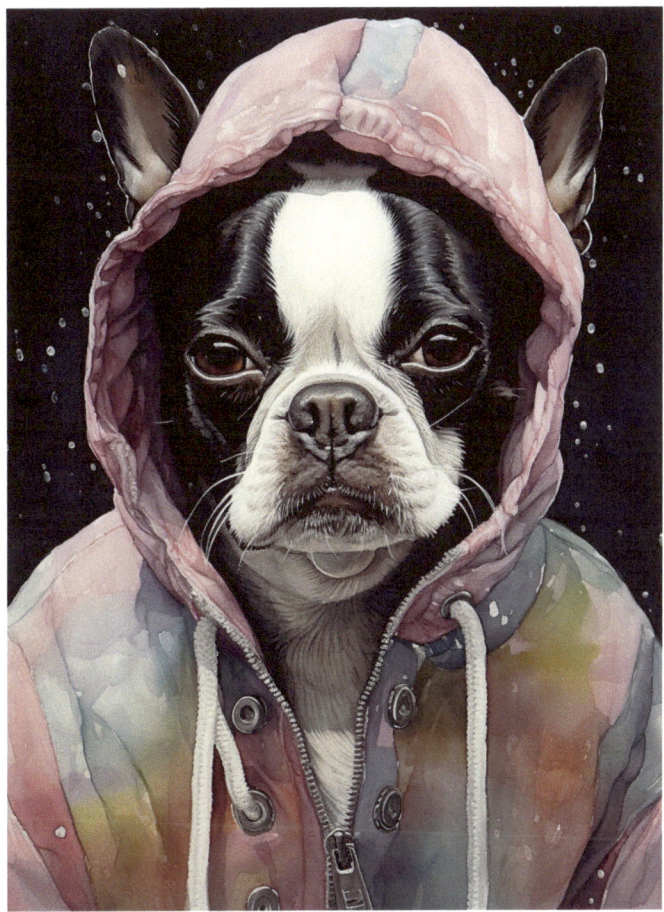

boston terrier watercolor painting, person, in the style of bubble goth, fantastic realism, irridescent, light brown and pink --v 5.2 --ar 3:4

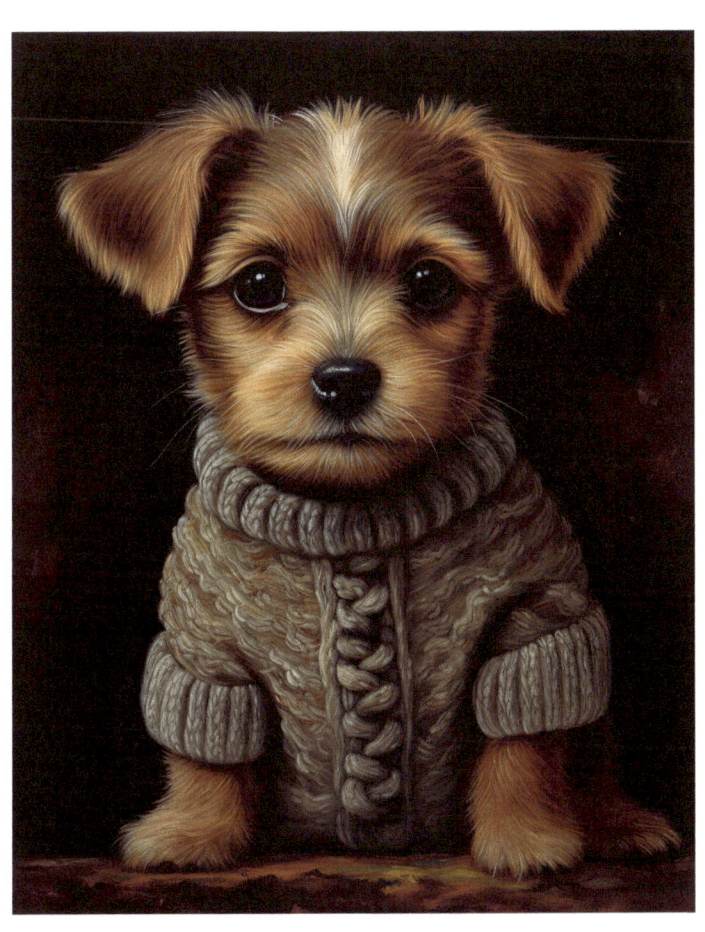

a really cute tiny puppy wearing a knitted sweater, pastel art --v 5.2 --ar 85:110

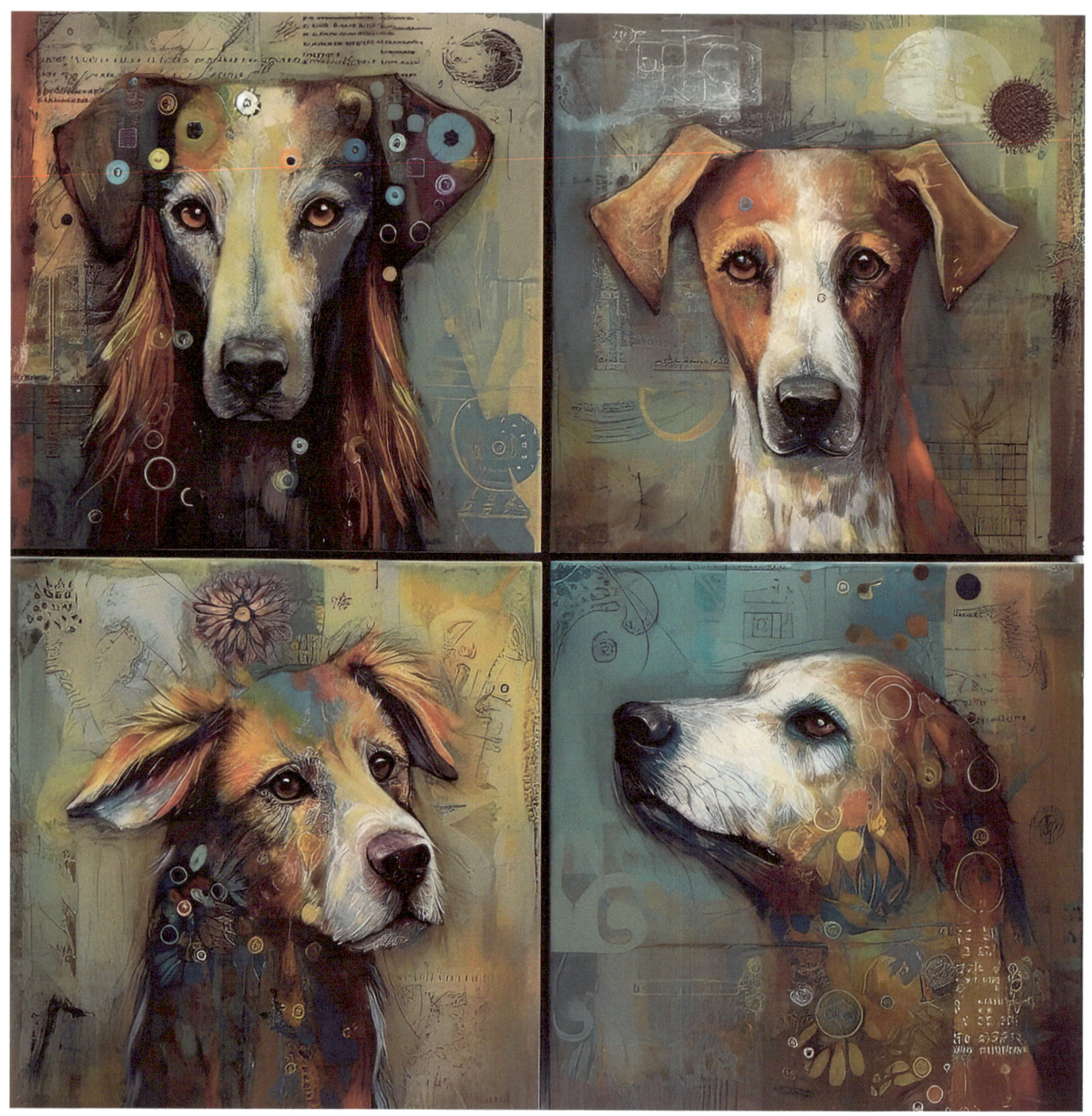

four small, colorful pictures of dogs, in the style of text-based mixed media, quirky expressionism, layered textures, shaped canvas, tanbi kei, i can't believe how beautiful this is
--v 5 --s 250 --ar 160:157

collaged boxer puppy sitting in an armchair, mixed media art made with tissue paper, magazine and newspaper clippings, oil paint, ink lines and fabric --v 5 --ar 85:110

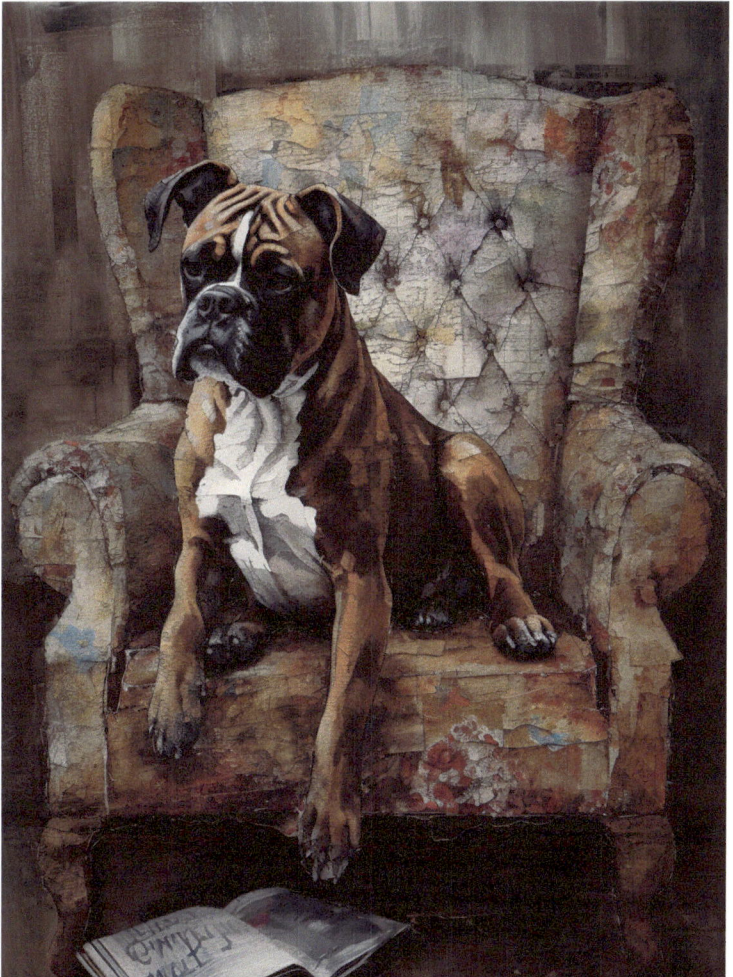

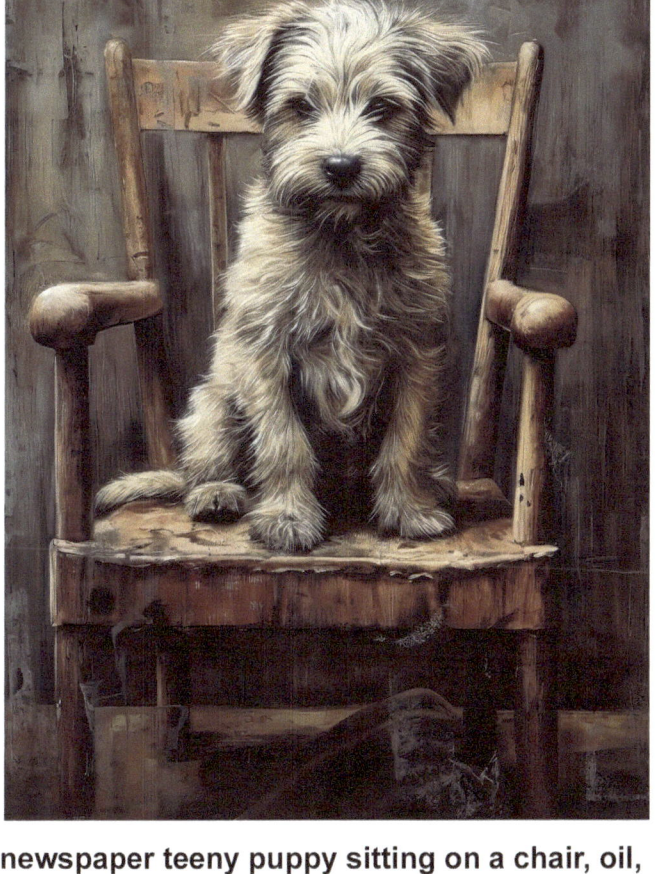

newspaper teeny puppy sitting on a chair, oil, --v 5.1 --ar 58:77

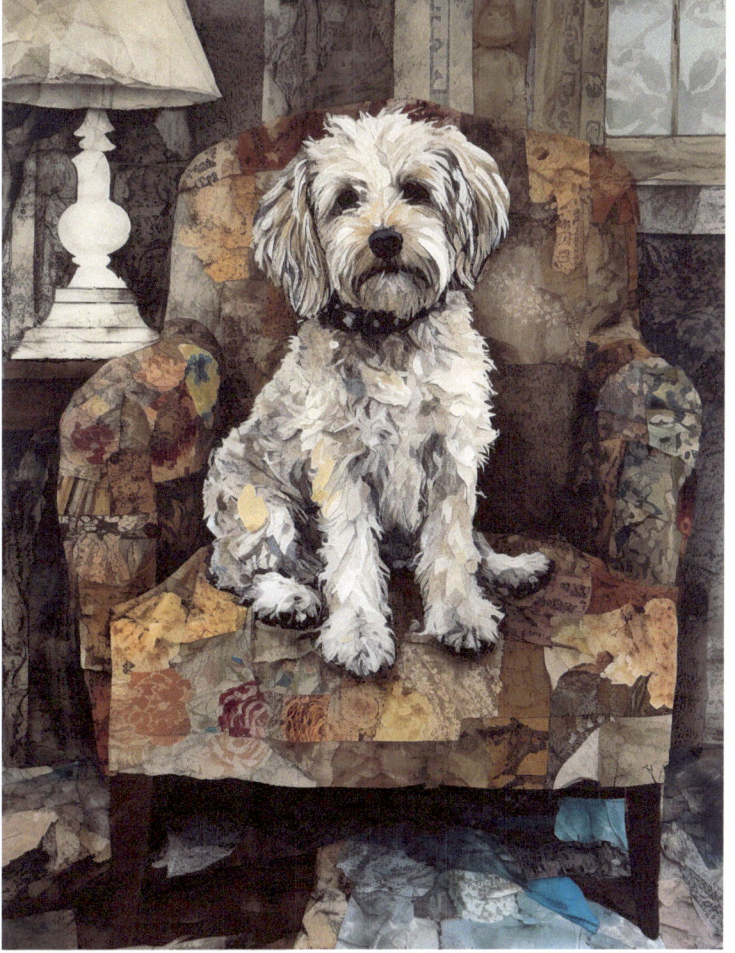

collaged labradoodle puppy sitting in an armchair, mixed media art made with tissue paper, magazine and newspaper clippings, oil paint, ink lines and fabric --v 5 --ar 85:110

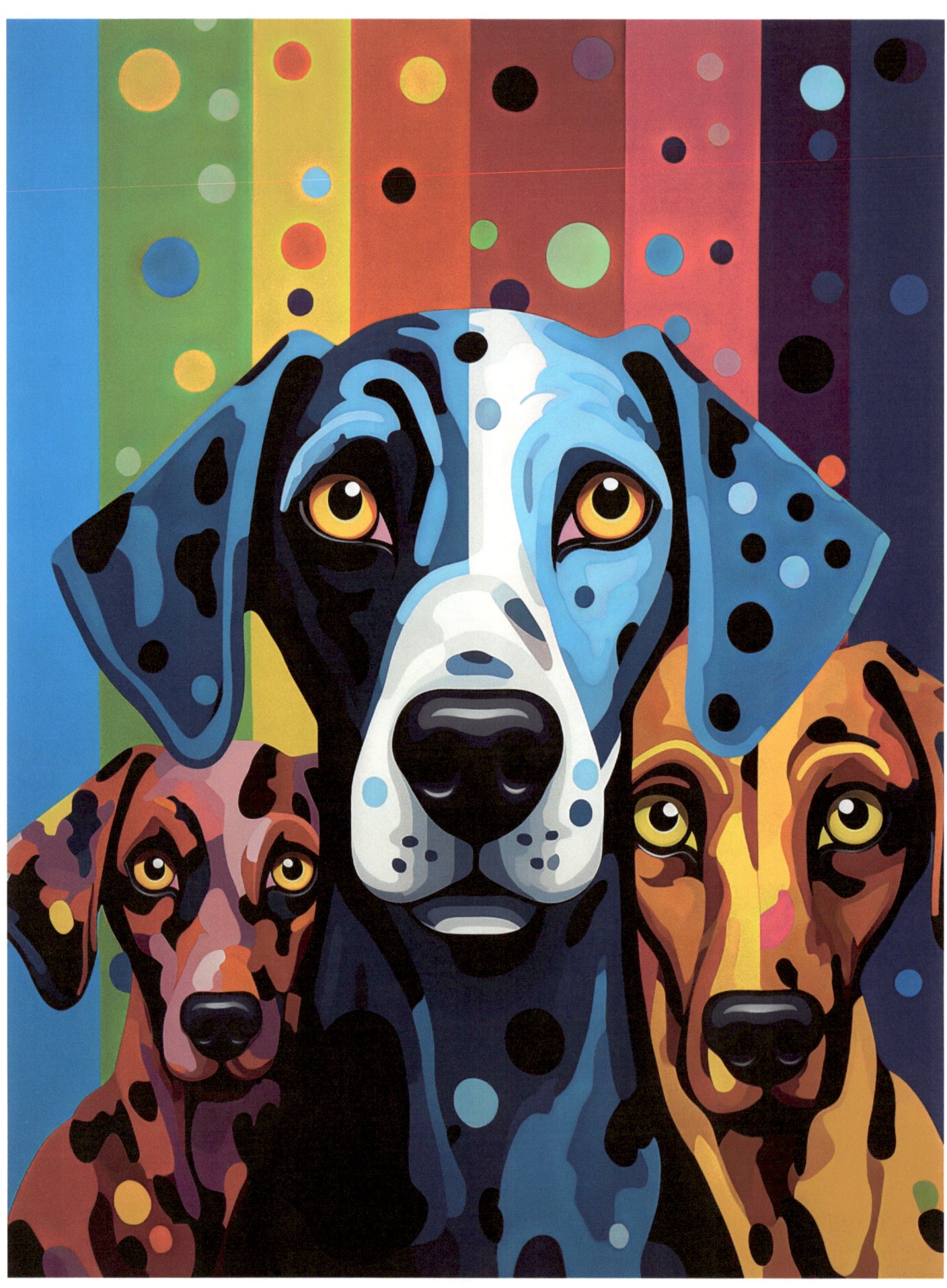

colorful dogs in the style of pop art graphic style, distinctive noses, airbrush art, dark white and dark black, whimsical cartoon-style, chiaroscuro portraitures --v 5.2 --ar 85:110

person artist painting a black and white dog, in the style of disturbingly whimsical, made of feathers, striped, furry art, himalayan art --v 5.2 --ar 27:28

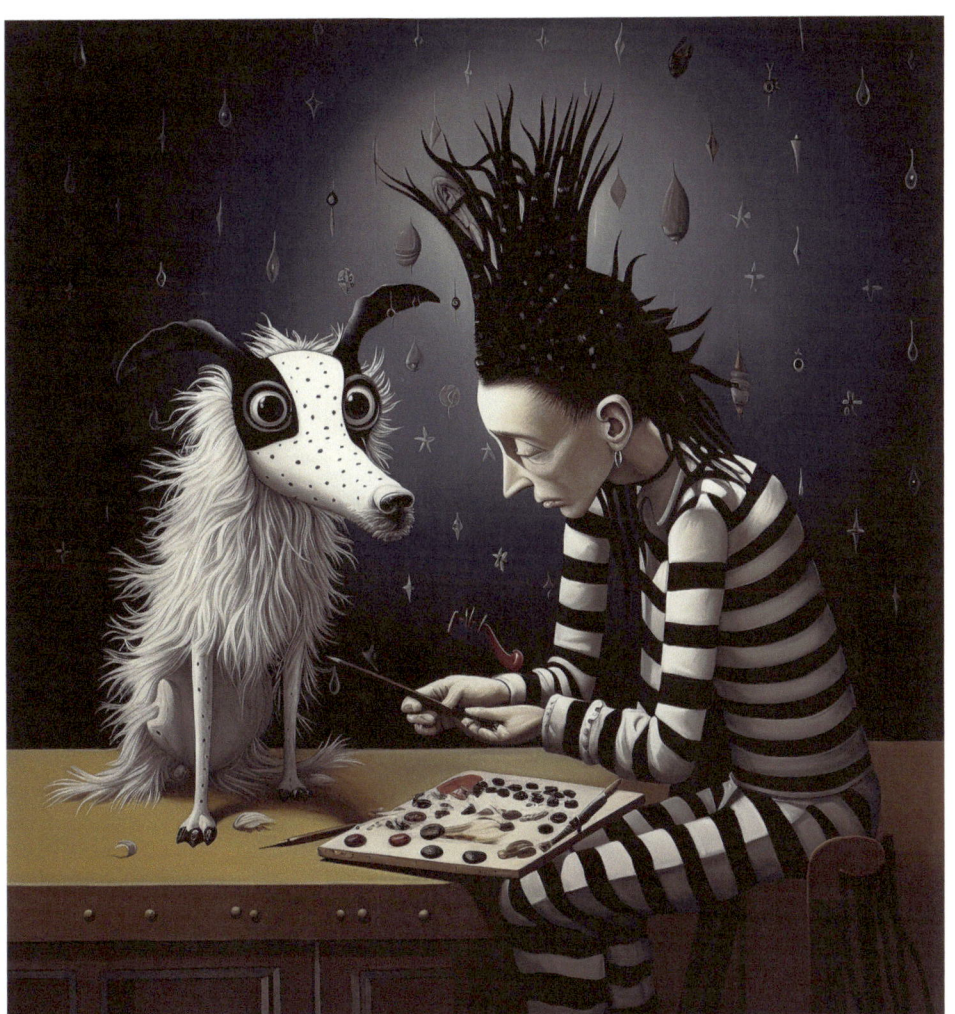

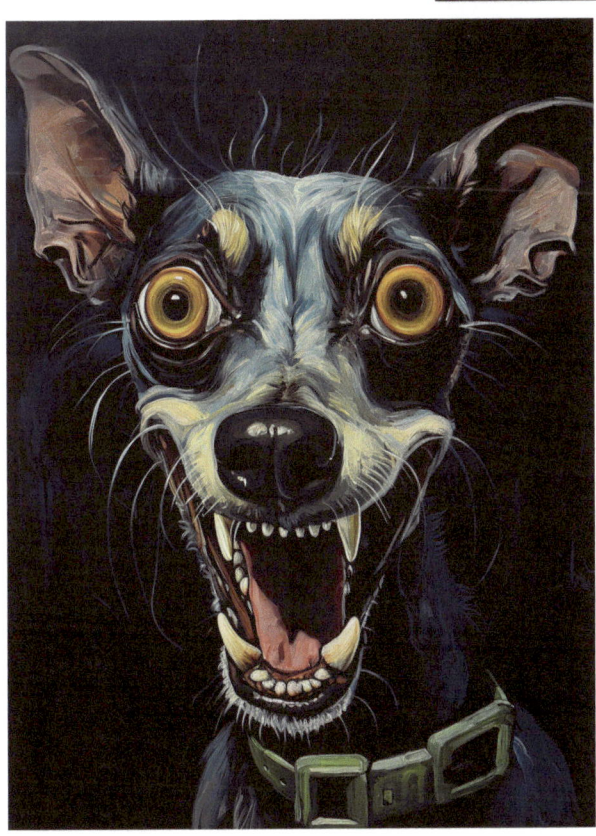

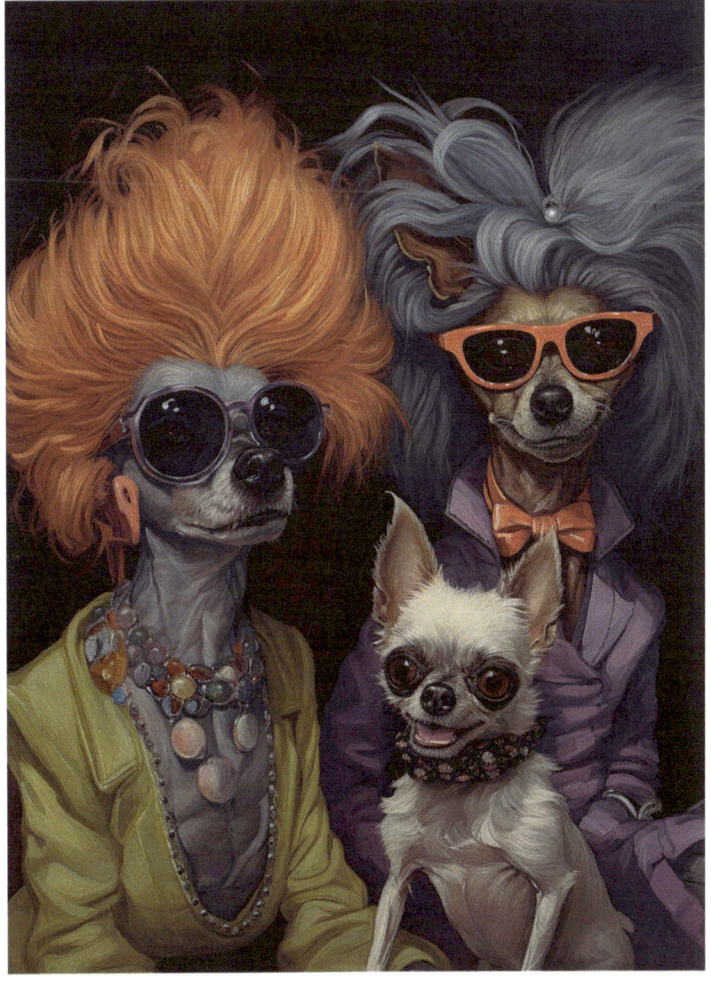

dog painting in the style of grotesque caricatures, precisionism influence, punk art, sharp/prickly, oku art, tumblewave, oil portraitures --v 5.2 --ar 37:50

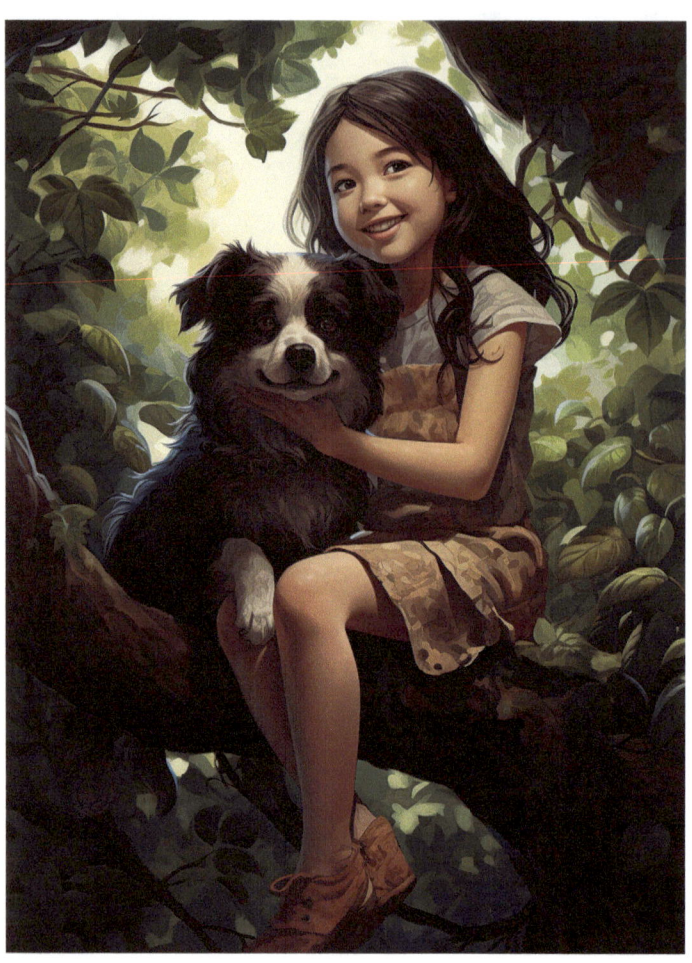

a girl and dog are holding each other in the tree, babycore --v 5.2 --ar 45:59

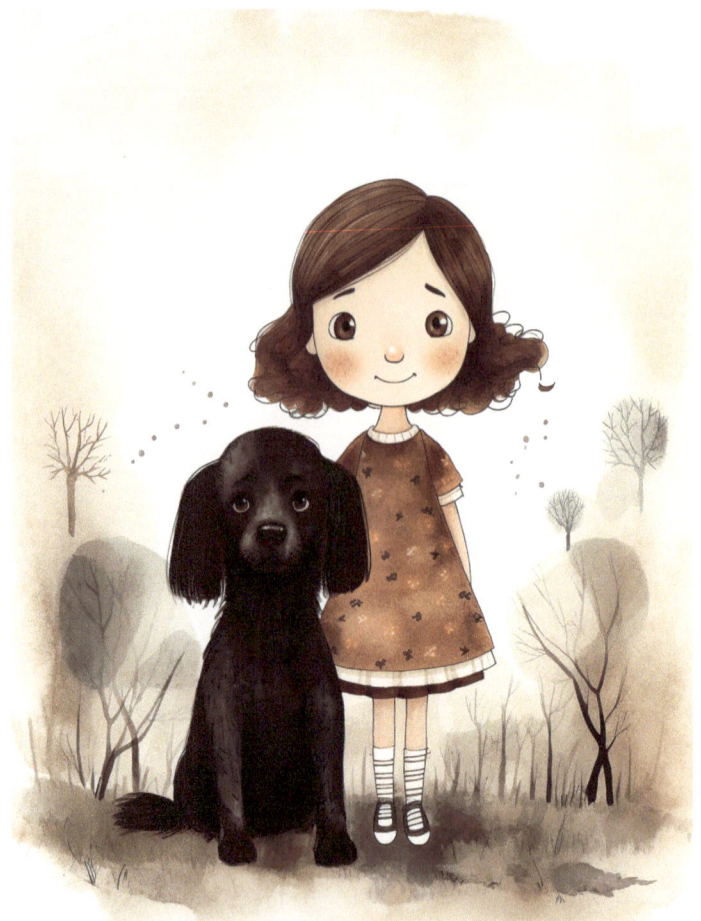

girl with brown hair and freckles with brown eyes, next to a sweet dog in the style of book illustration --v 5.2 --ar 85:110

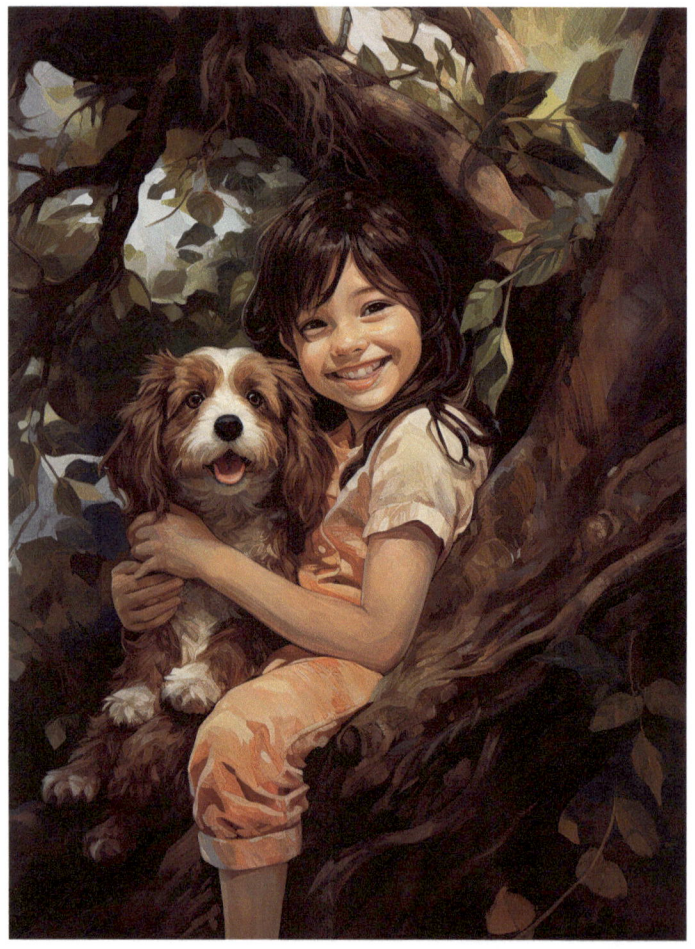

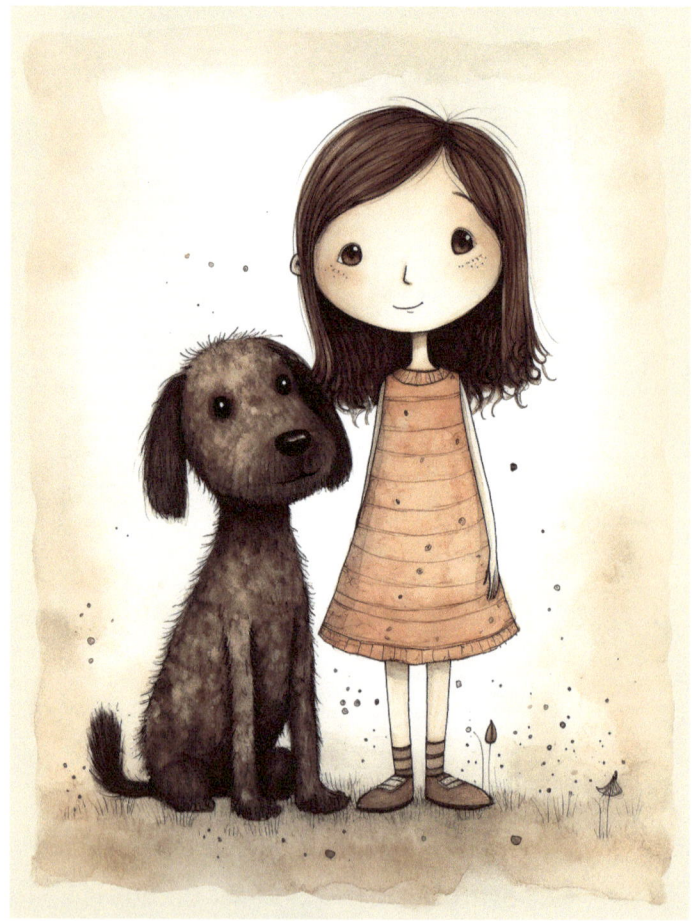

a dog painting on paper, in the style of furry art, trick of the eye paintings, light pink and turquoise, striped painting, colorful caricature --v 5.2 --ar 85:110

two dogs of different breeds are shown side by side, pastel goth, digital expressionism, avocadopunk, draftpunk --v 5.2 --ar 93:125

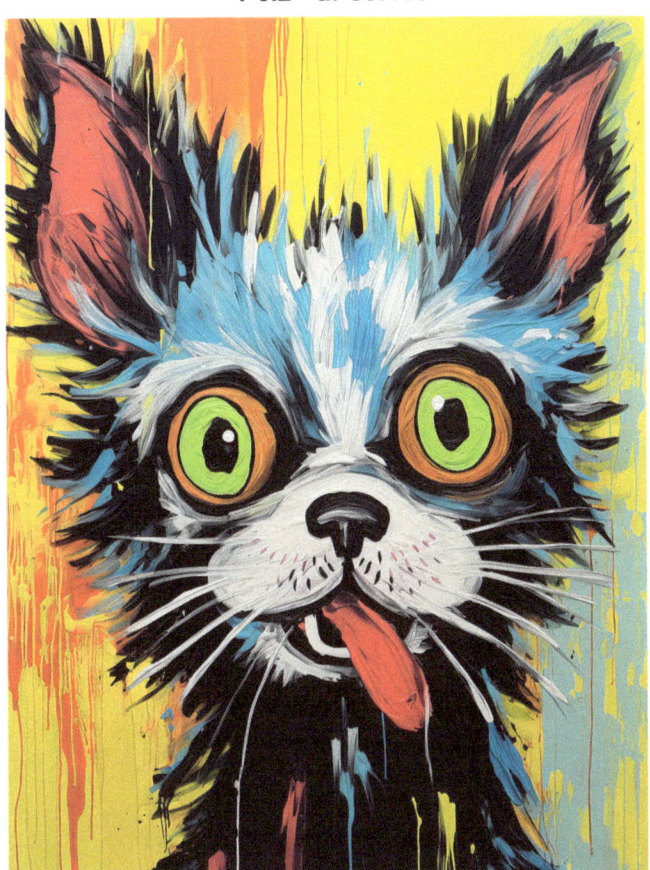

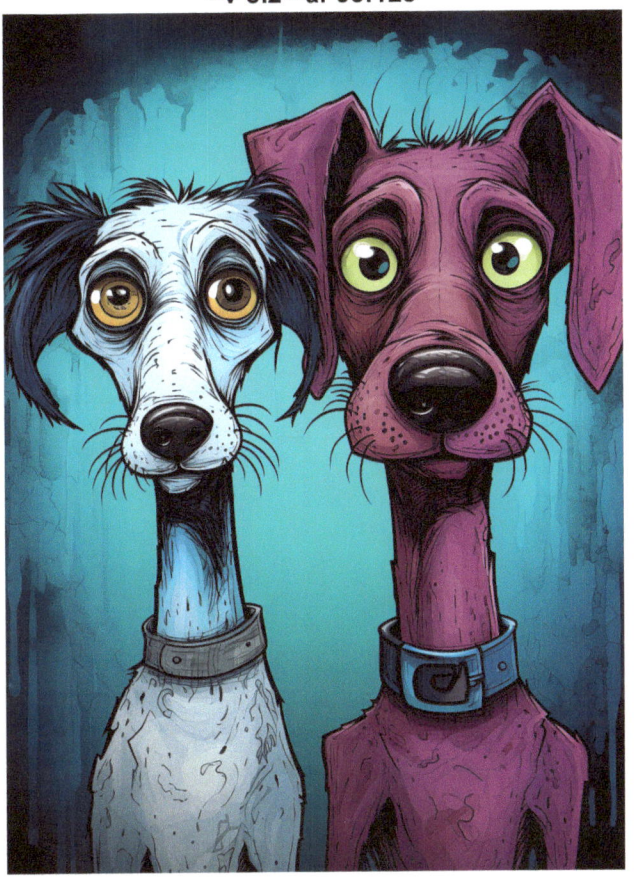

a row of cute miniature silly quirky poodles, a collage of mixed media art made with tissue paper, magazine and newspaper clippings, oil paint, pencil lines and fabric, in the style of playful surrealism, whimsical --v 5.2 --ar 3:2 --style raw

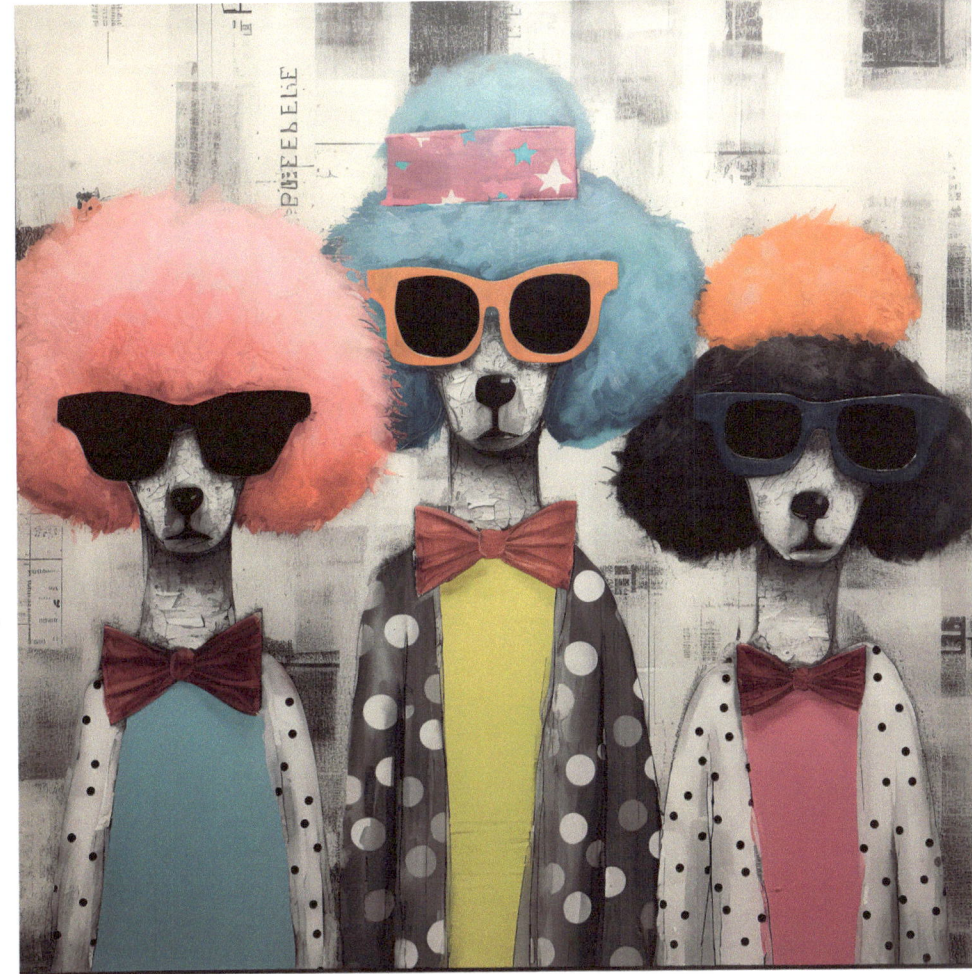

The main prompt stays the same, the name of the artist goes between the brackets { }

style of {artist} scruffy white dog running on the moon,
in a dark night, whimsical illustration --v 5.1 --s 950

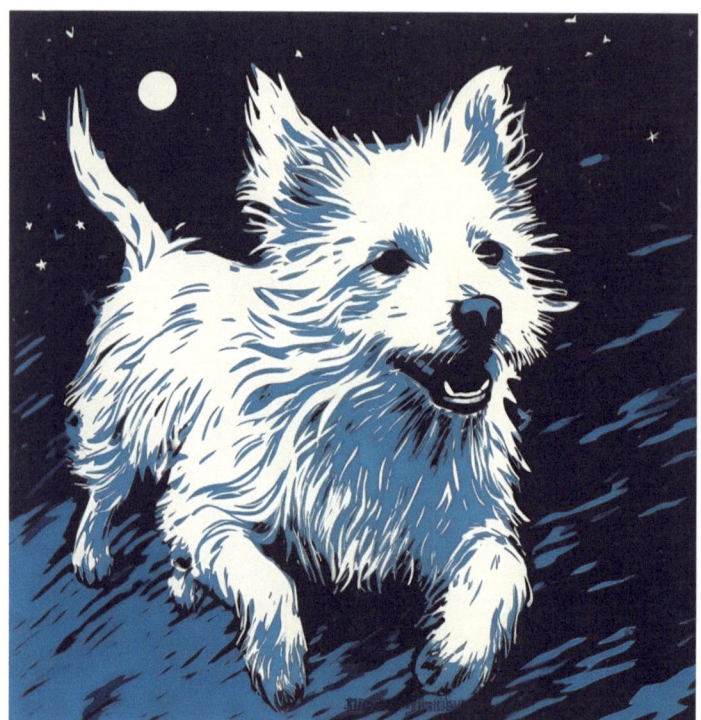

Andy Warhol

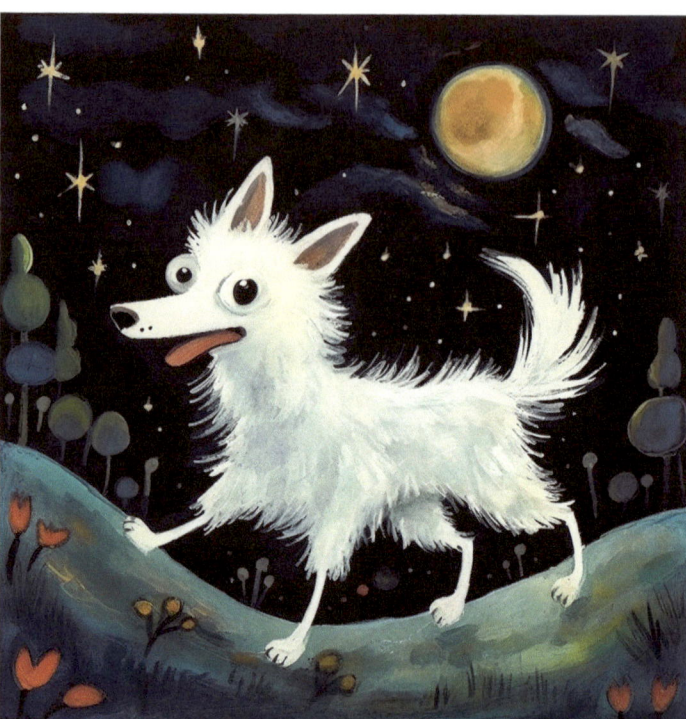

Frida Kahlo

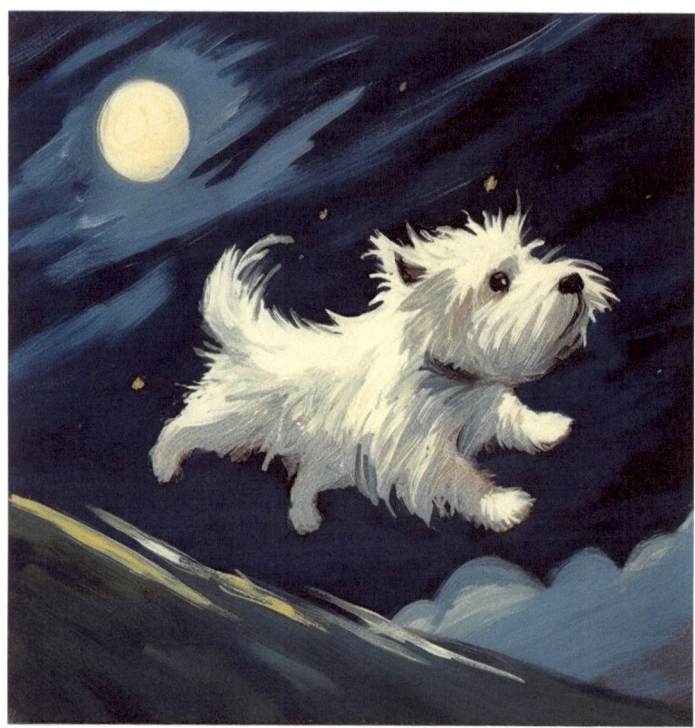

Edward Hopper

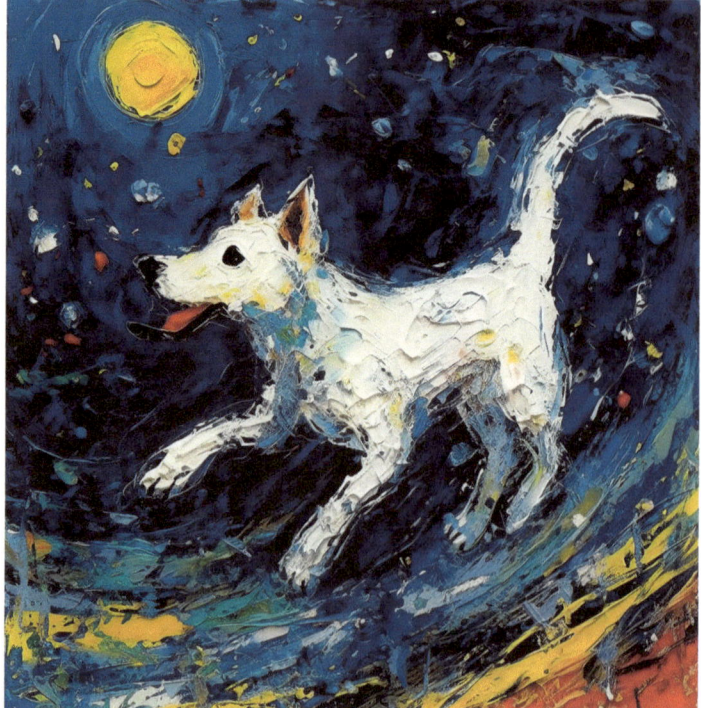

Jackson Pollock

Pablo Picasso

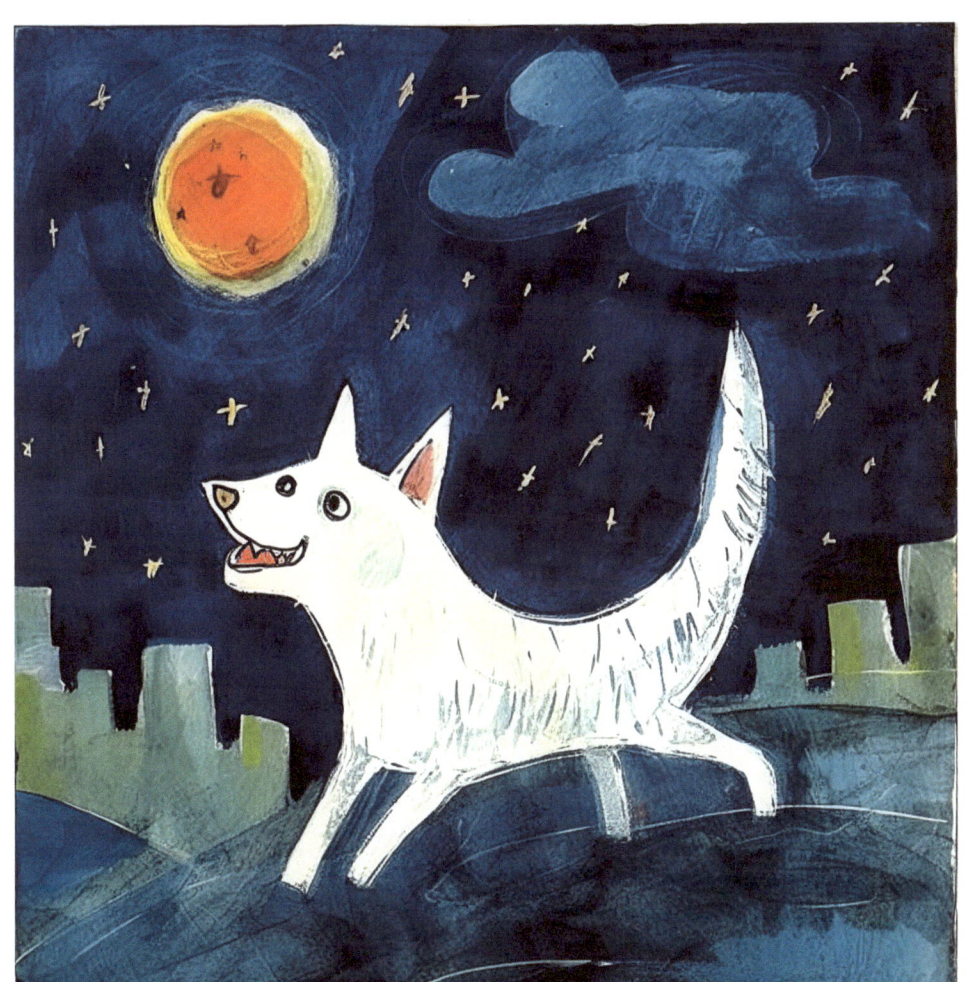

Marc Chagall

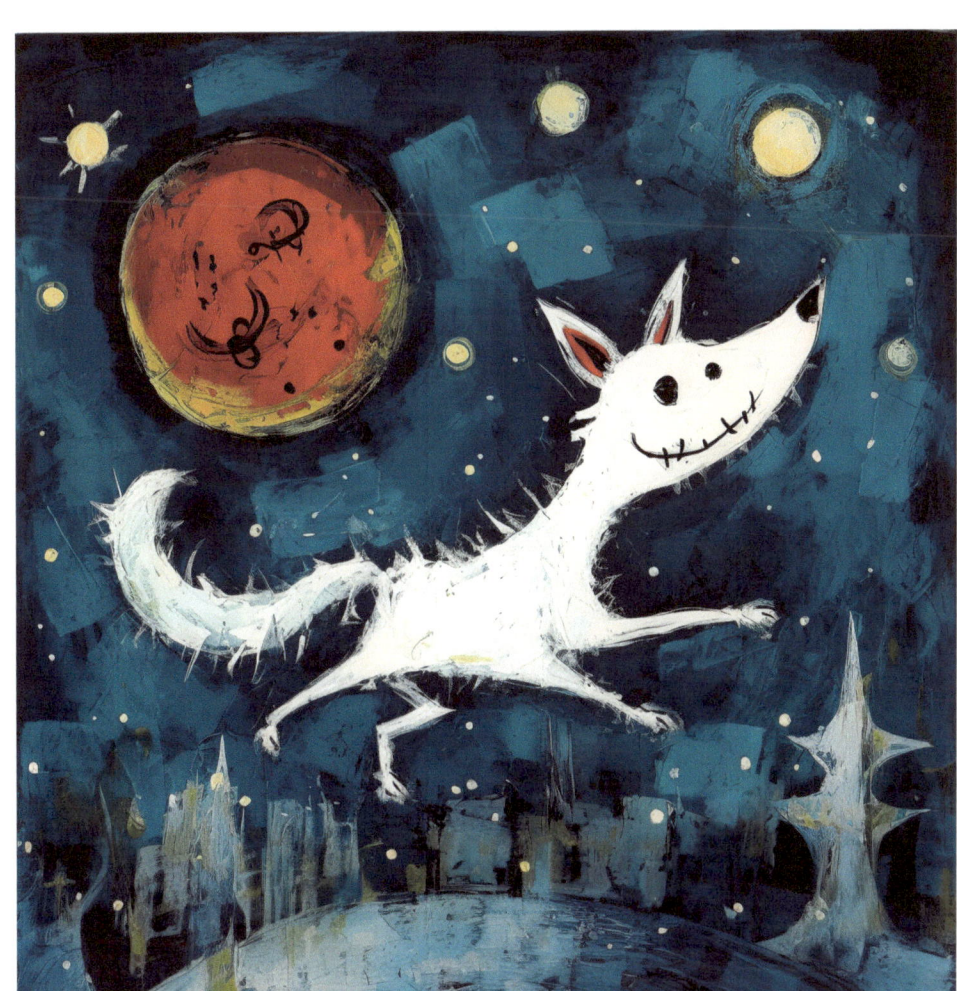

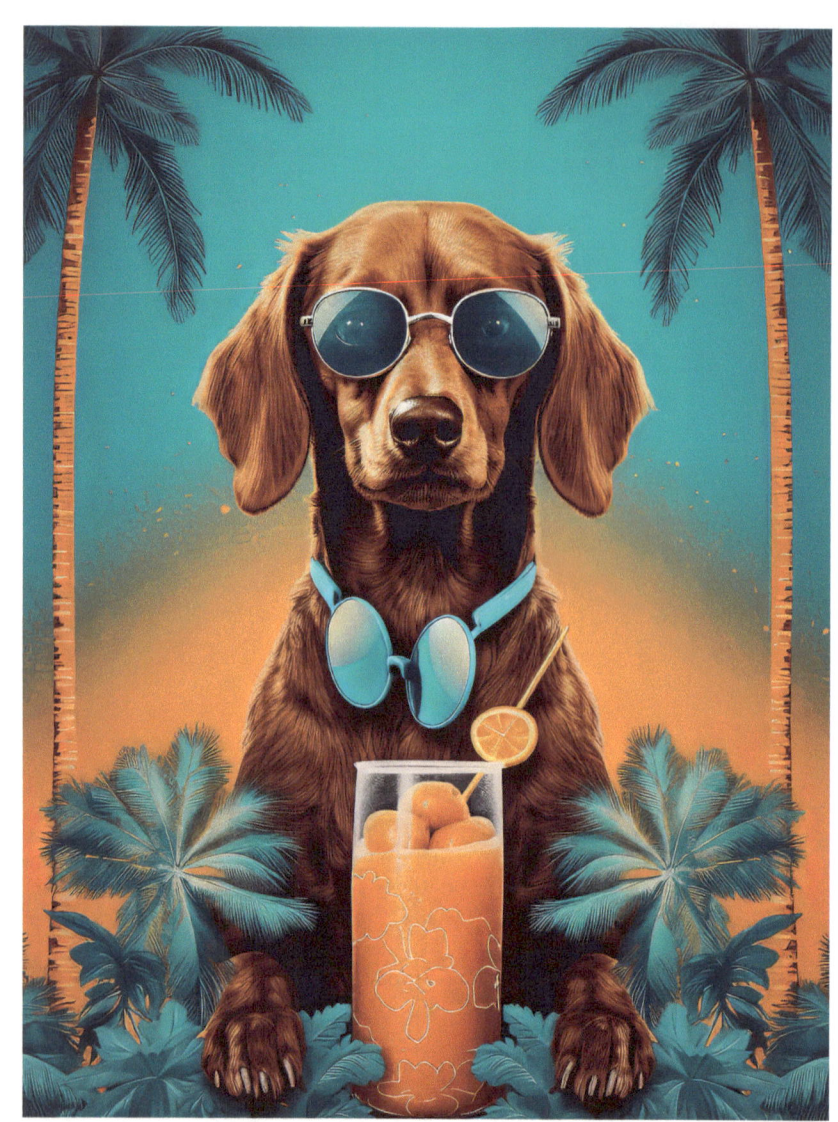

dog on sand wearing sunglasses and drinking a cocktail, in the style of dark orange and dark azure, enigmatic tropics, verdadism
--v 5.2 --ar 85:110 --s 250

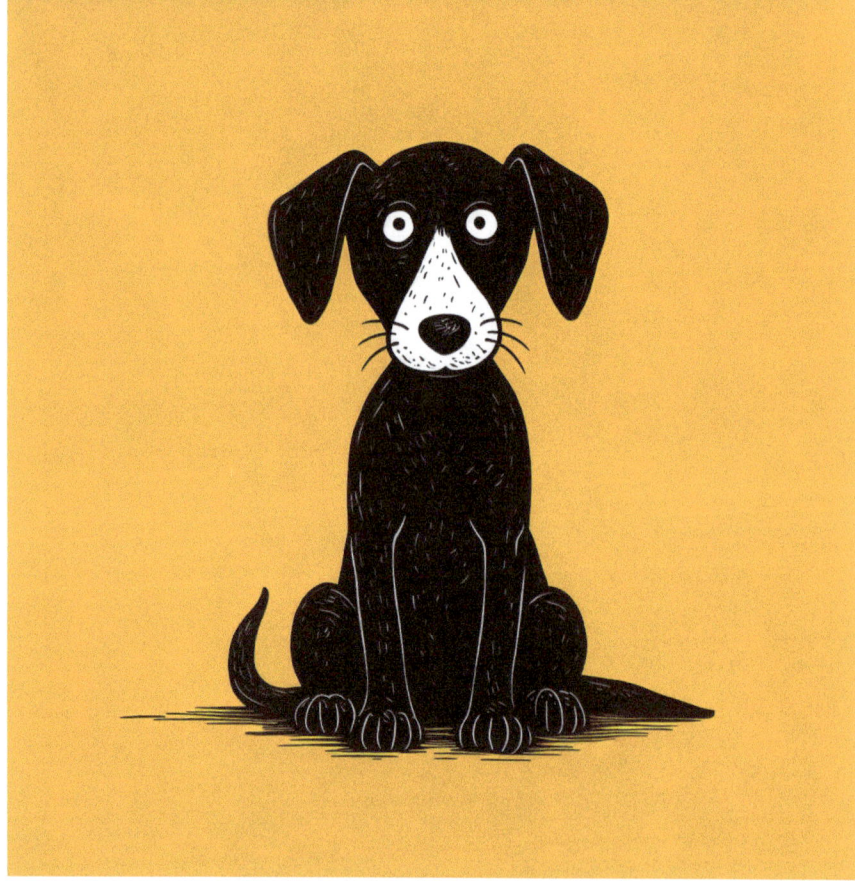

a black dog, pointy ears, in the style of Roger Hargreaves illustrations, cute pointy ears, looking sad --v 5.2 --s 750 --s 250 surfer dog canvas painting, classic american cars, playful and whimsical depictions of animals, petcore, soft, romantic scenes --v 5.1 --ar 16:9 --s 250

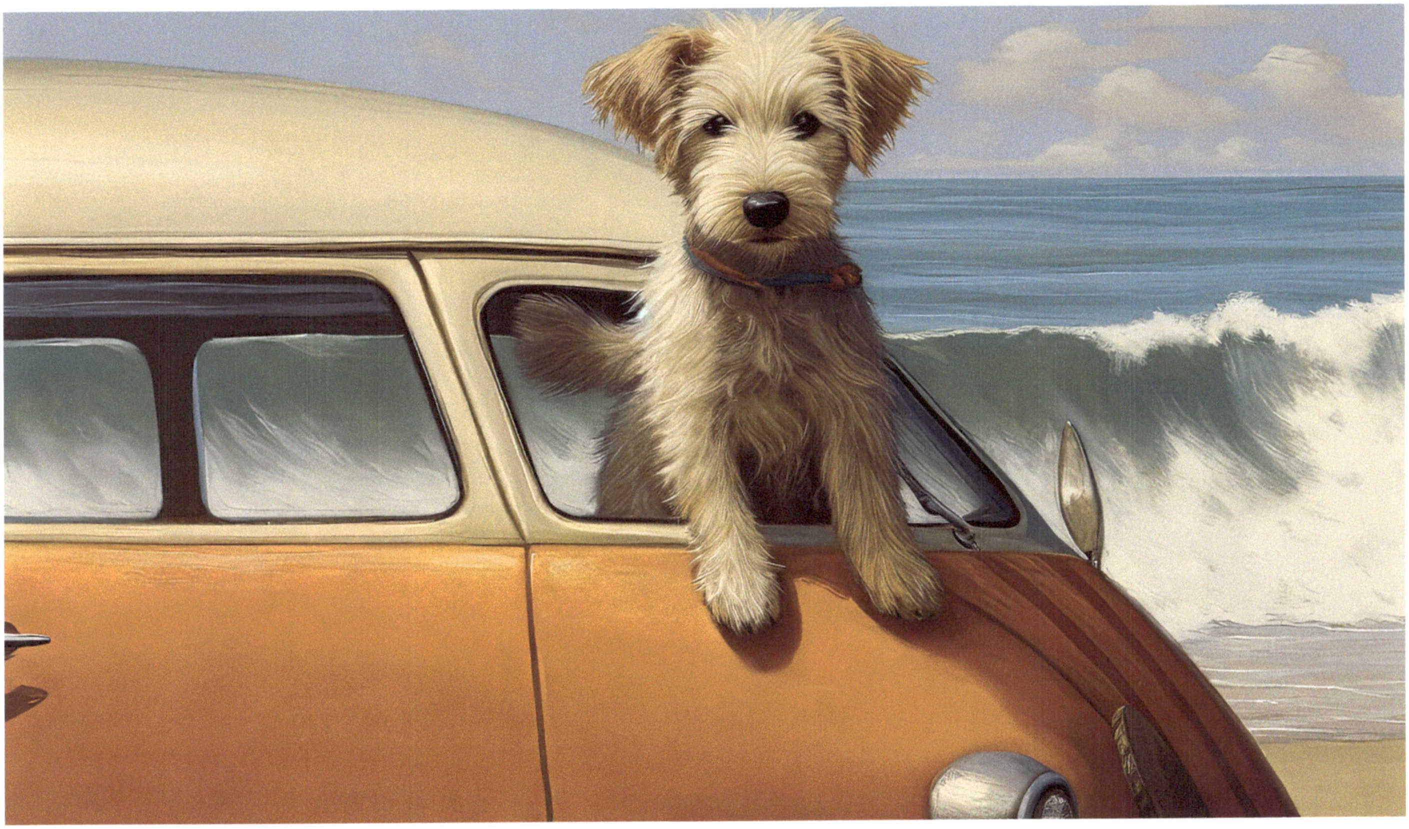

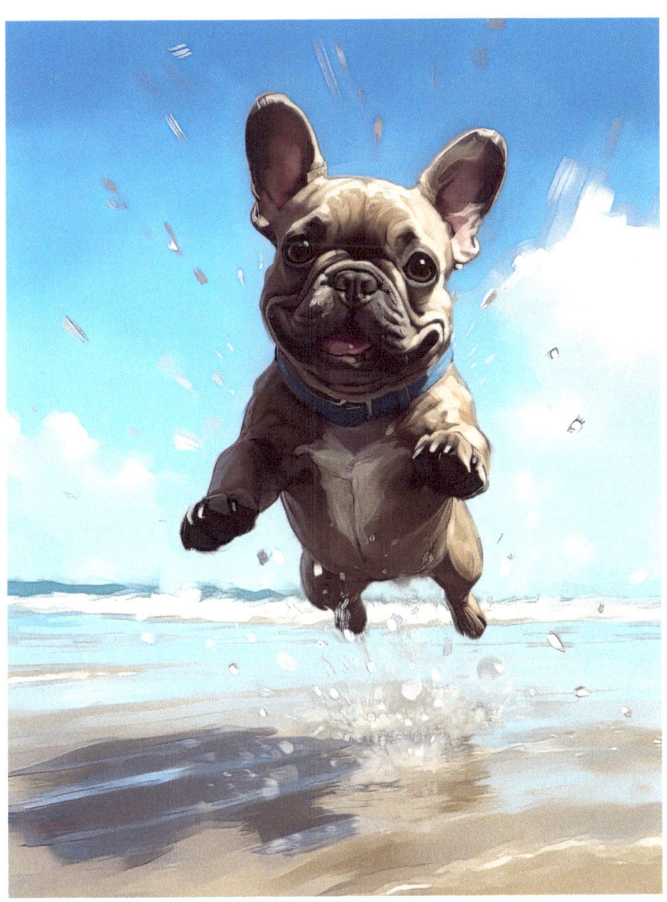

french bulldog puppy playing on the beach, detailed character, high resolution --v 5.2 --ar 85:110 --s 250 --style raw

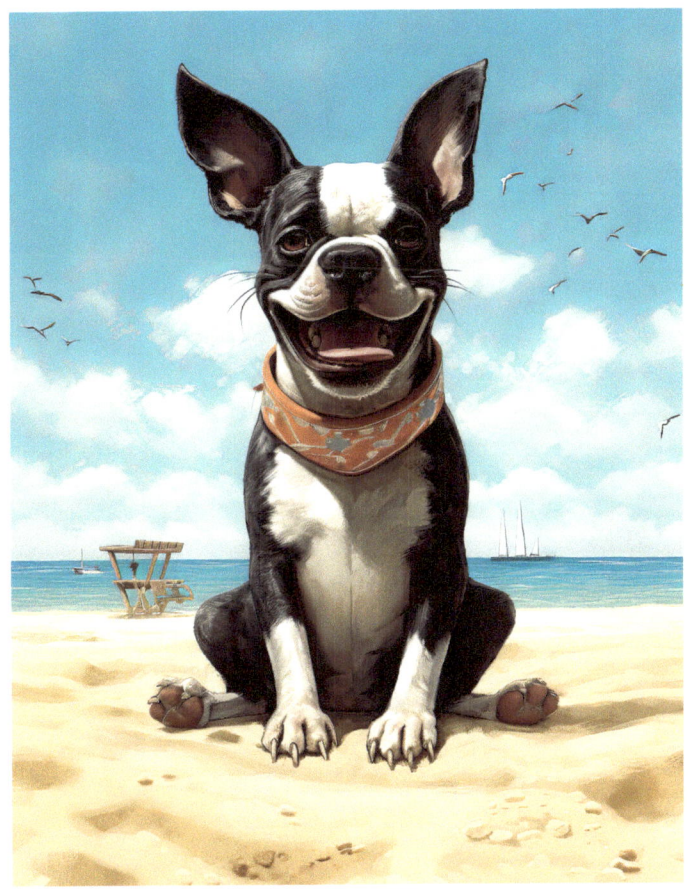

beach sitting dog on sand, in the style of cartoon realism, pixel perfect, traditional oil-painting, illustration, wimmelbilder --v 5.2 --ar 4:5 --s 250

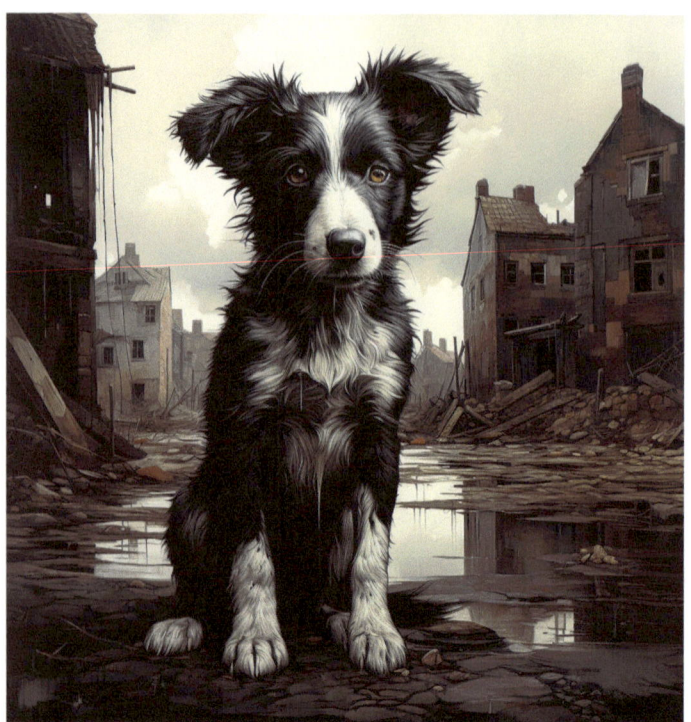

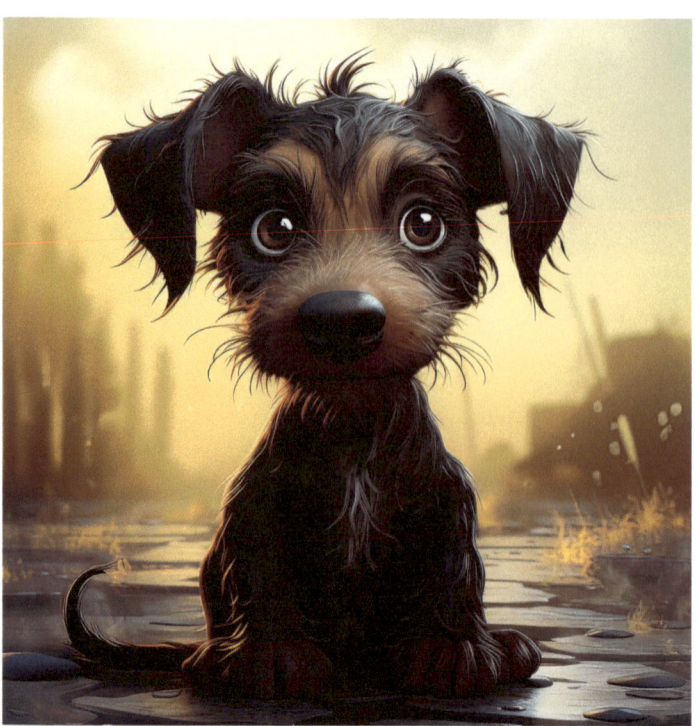

a black and white dog standing on a street, decaying landscapes, brooding cityscapes, young british artists, soggy --v 5.2 --s 250

a cute little cartoon dog with short hair, in the style of whimsical realism, whimsical children's book illustrator, disney animation --v 5.2 --s 250

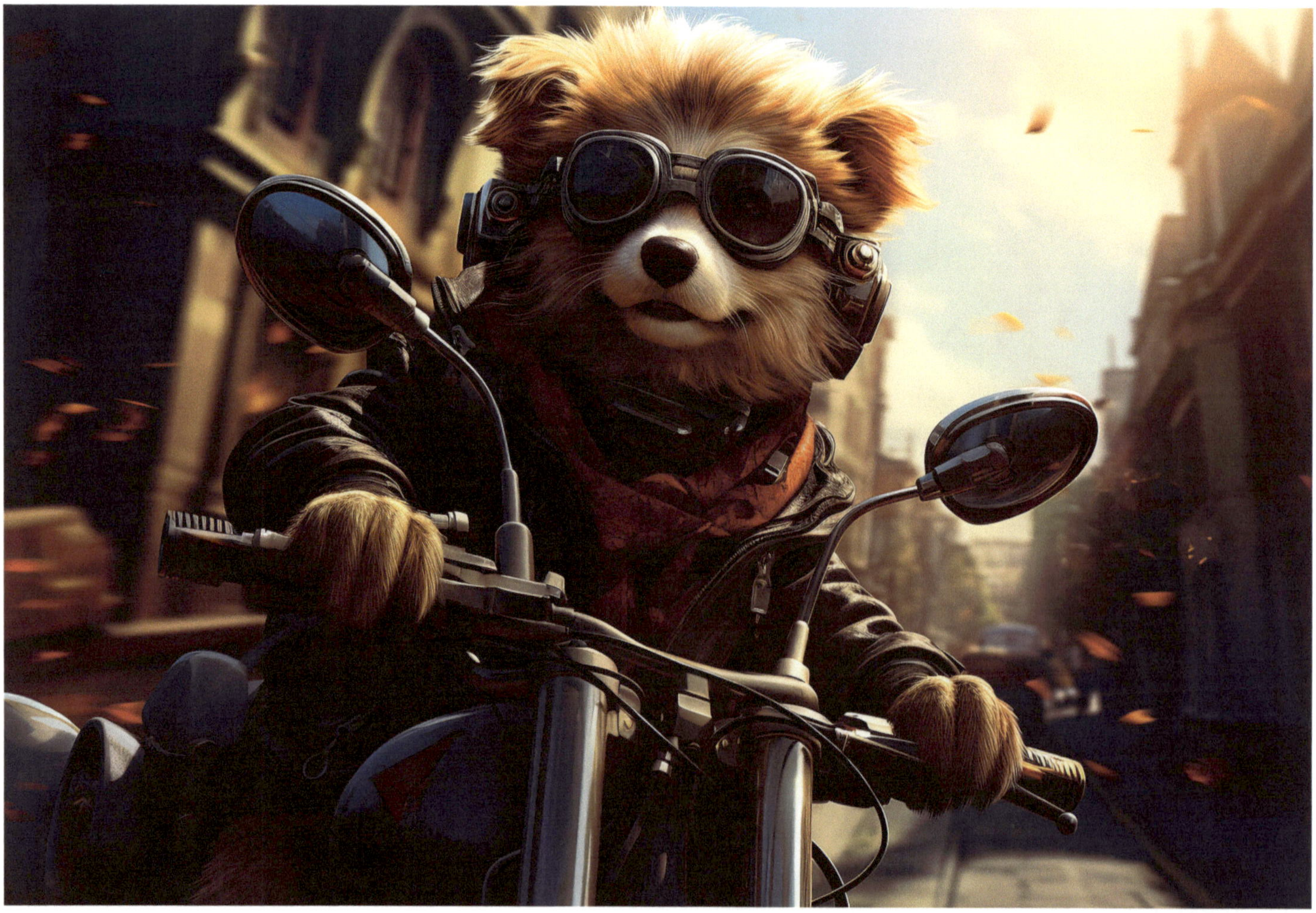

a cute puppy dog is riding a motorcycle through the street, in the style of red and brown, kawaiipunk, uniformly staged images, hd, caninecore --v 5.2 --s 250 --ar 3:2

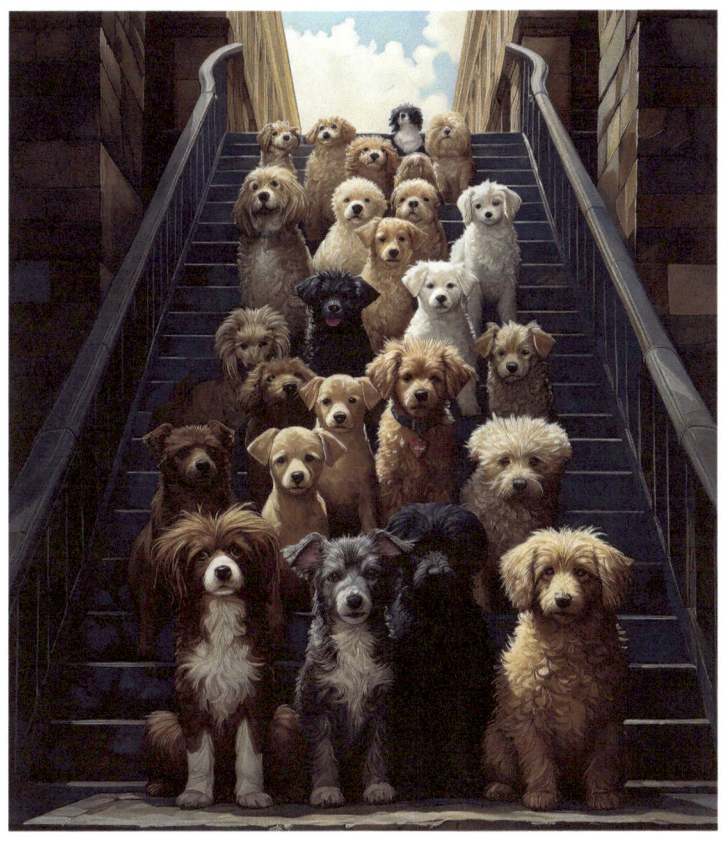

small dogs on steps looking at someone from afar, in the style of dark indigo and dark brown, poodlepunk --v 5.2 --s 250

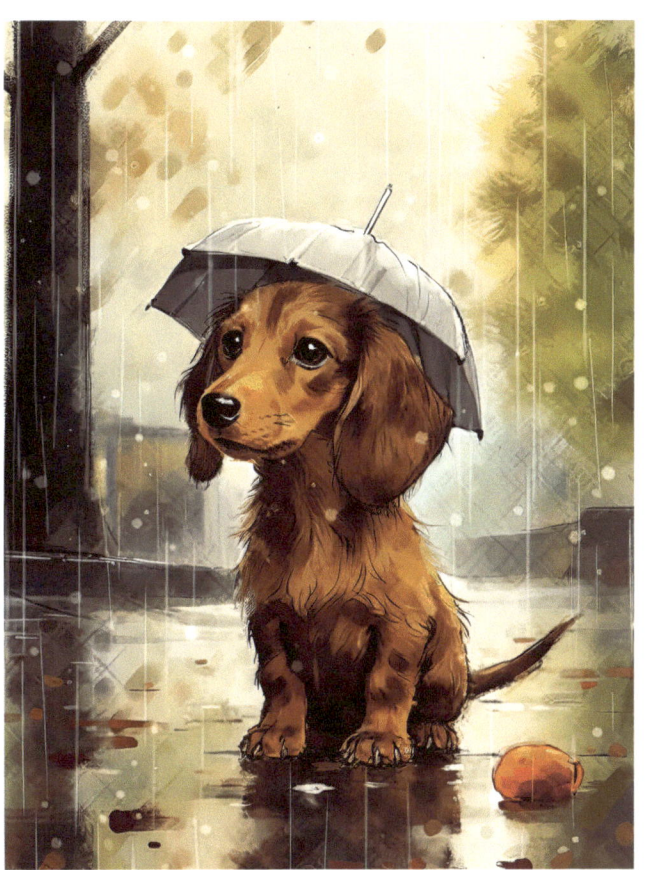

watercolor dachshund puppy, heavy rain, cute 2d illustration, urban sketch --v 5 --ar 85:110 --style raw

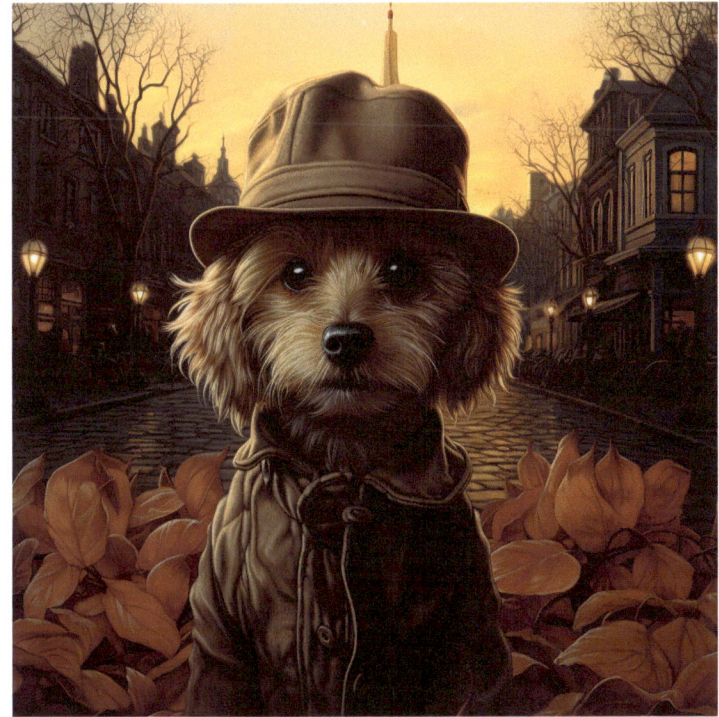

an animal in a hat wearing a hat, in the style of mark brooks, poodlepunk, street scene, smooth and shiny --v 5.2 --s 250

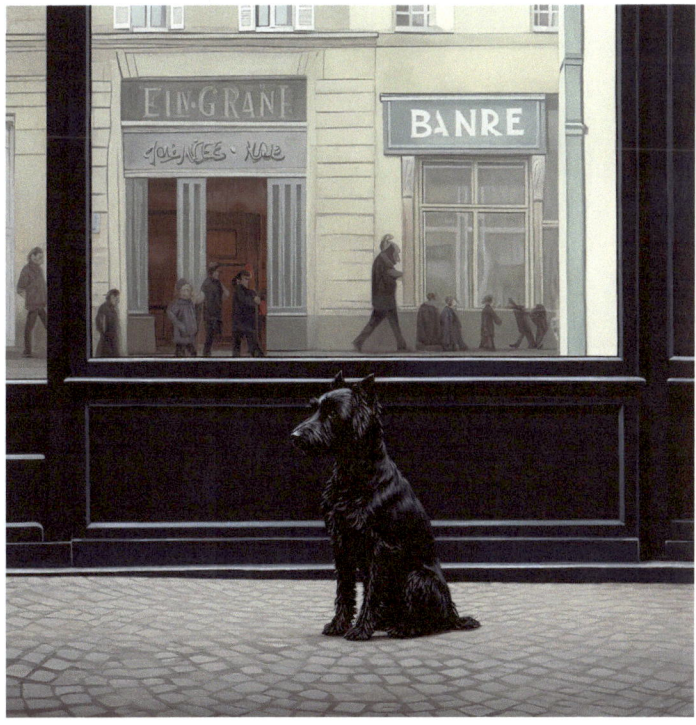

style of Rene Magritte, small black dog waiting outside a shop in Paris --v 5.1 --s 50

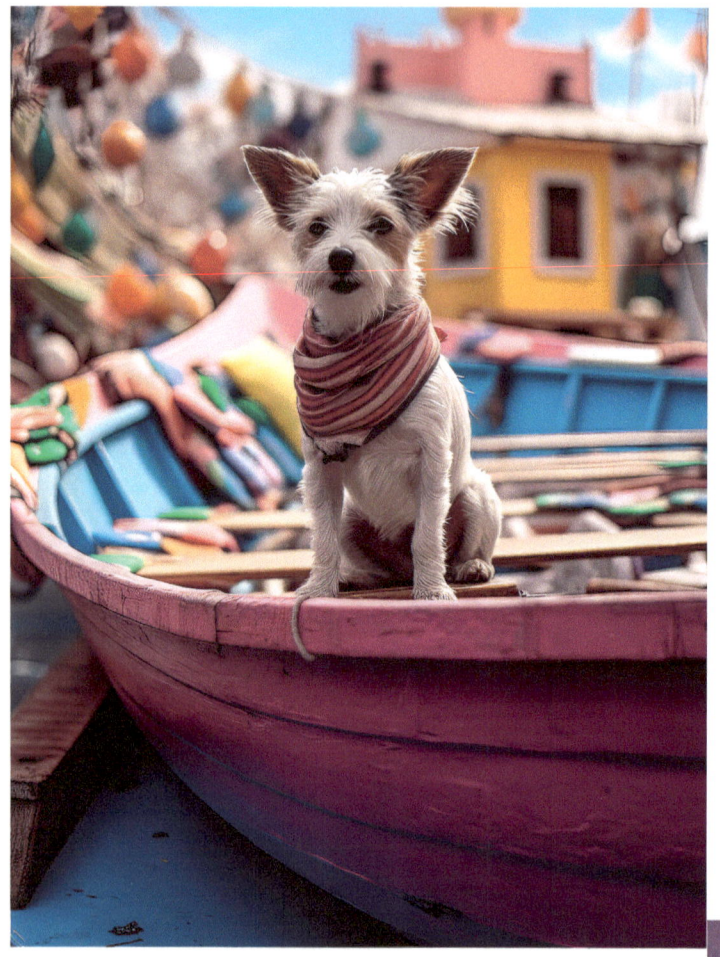

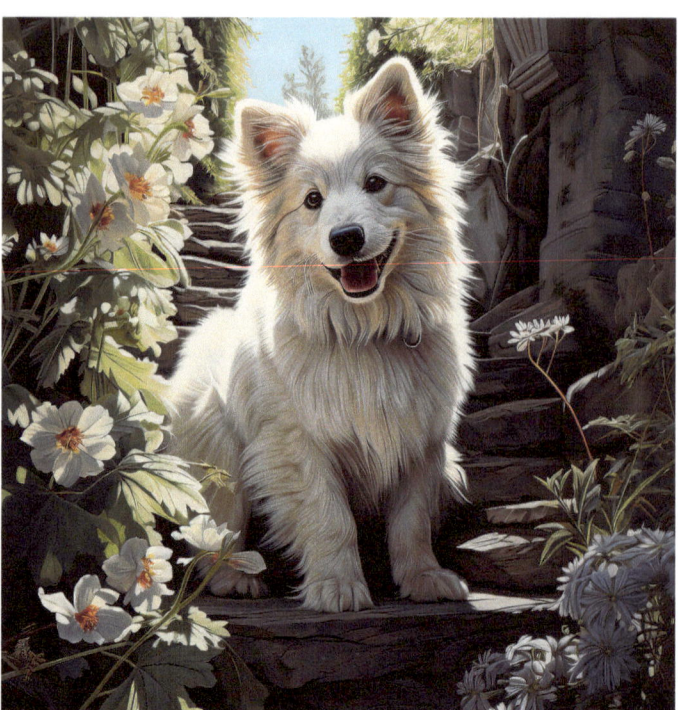

a flocked dog sitting on a stone path, in the style of airbrush art, colorful gardens, realistic color schemes, himalayan art, holotone printing, furry art --v 5.2 --s 250

small dog sitting on a boat near colorful boats at the beach, photobash, warmcore --v 5.2 --ar 85:110 --s 250

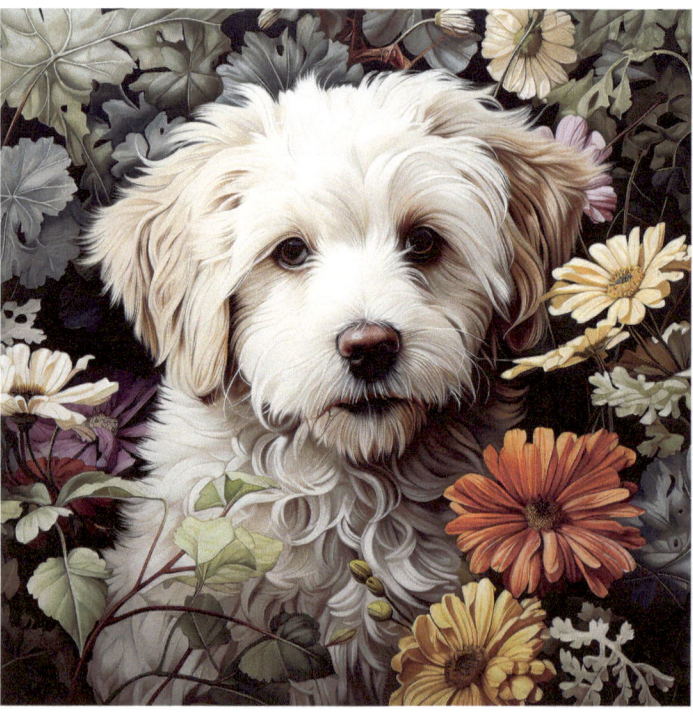

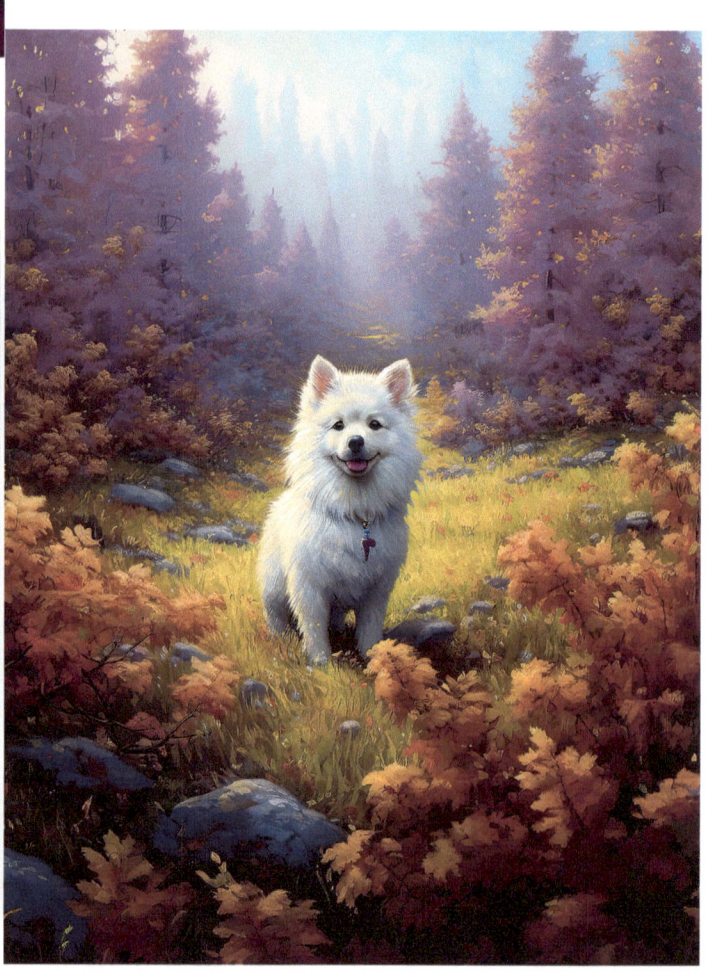

a drawing with flowers and a dog, style of realistic watercolors, cute and colorful, dye-transfer, detailed miniatures, wimmelbilder --v 5.2 --s 250

a small dog standing in a field full of purple bushes and yellow trees, delicately rendered landscapes --v 5.2 --ar 85:110

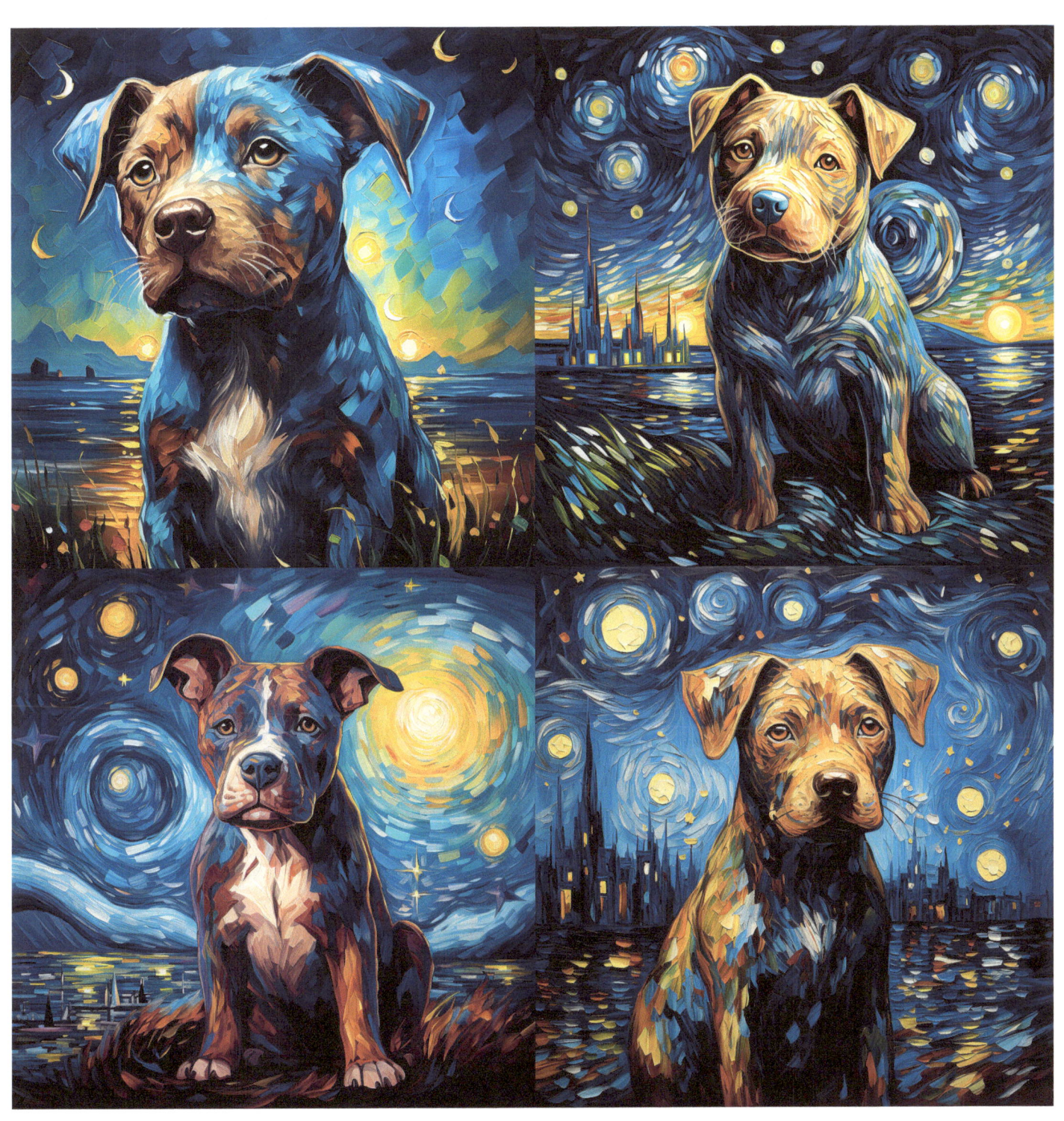

style of van gogh, cute pitbull puppy --v 5.2 --s 250

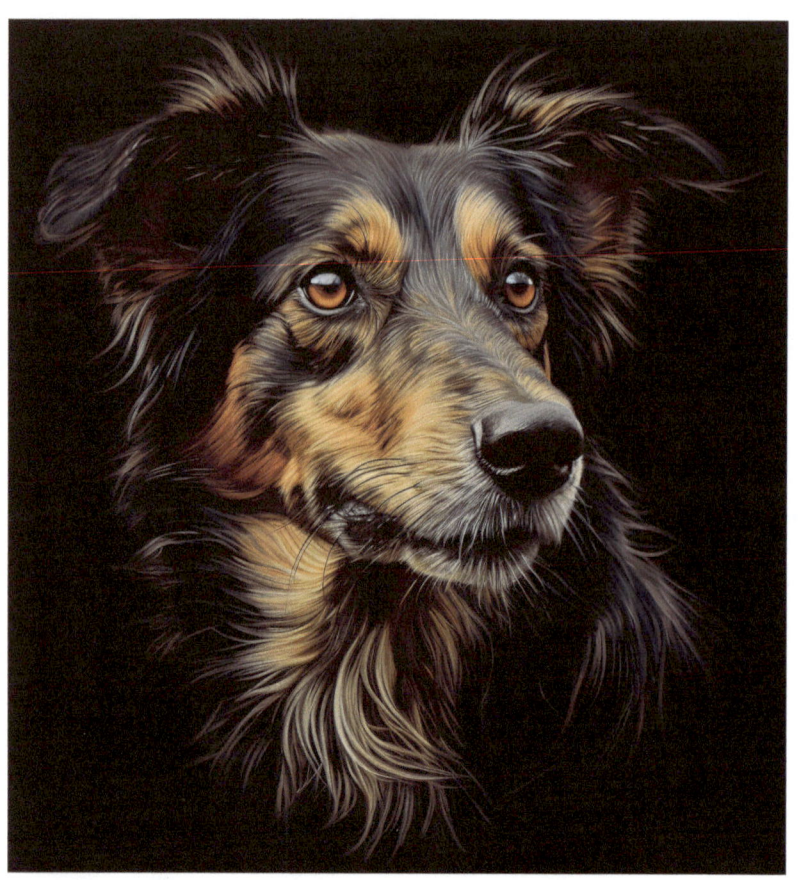

pastel sketch of jonah dog by stevie, in the style of wildlife art, black background, realistic oil portraits, dark amber and black --v 5.2

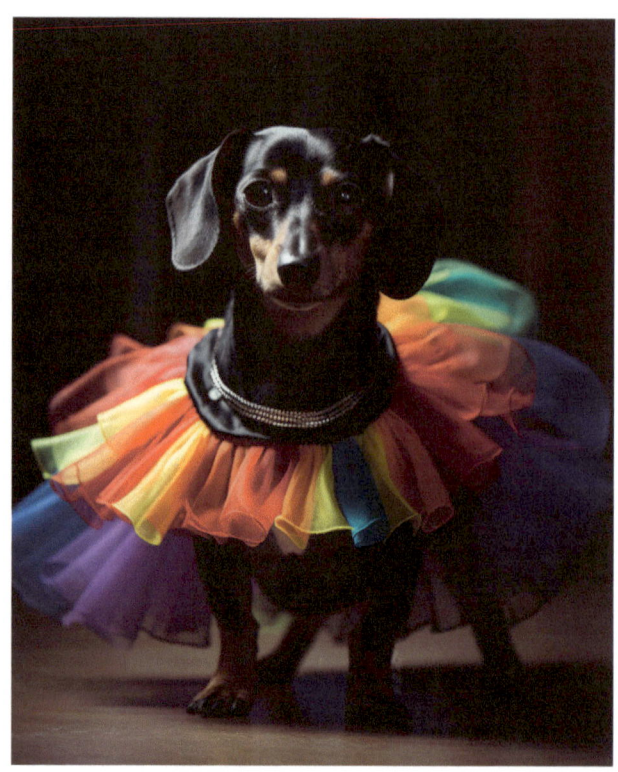

rainbow tutu dancer dachshund, in the style of kuromicore, inventive, naïve, velvia --v 5.2 --s 250

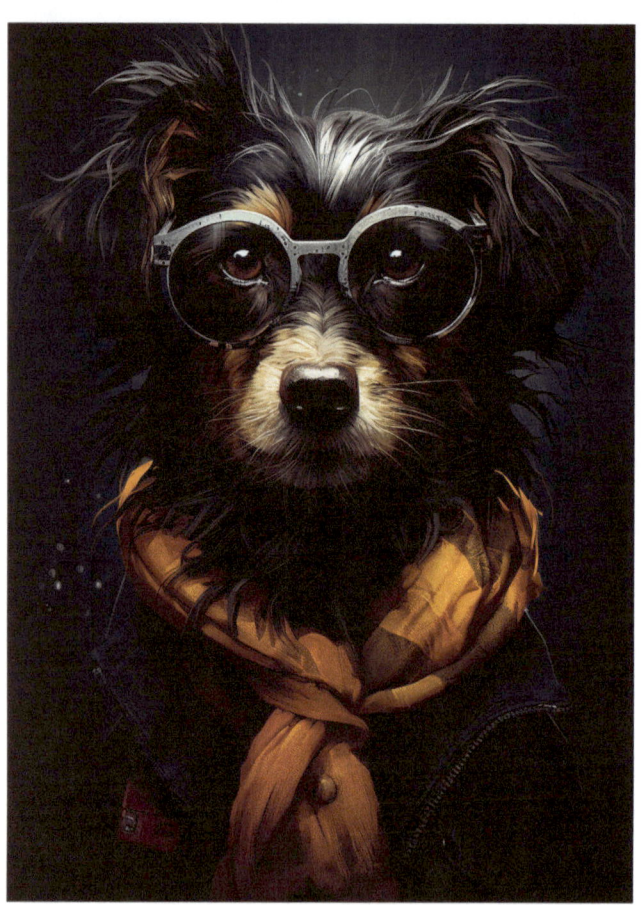

a small dog who is wearing glasses with a scarf, in the style of digital art, industrial-punk, portrait paintings, charming characters, studio portrait --v 5.2 --s 250

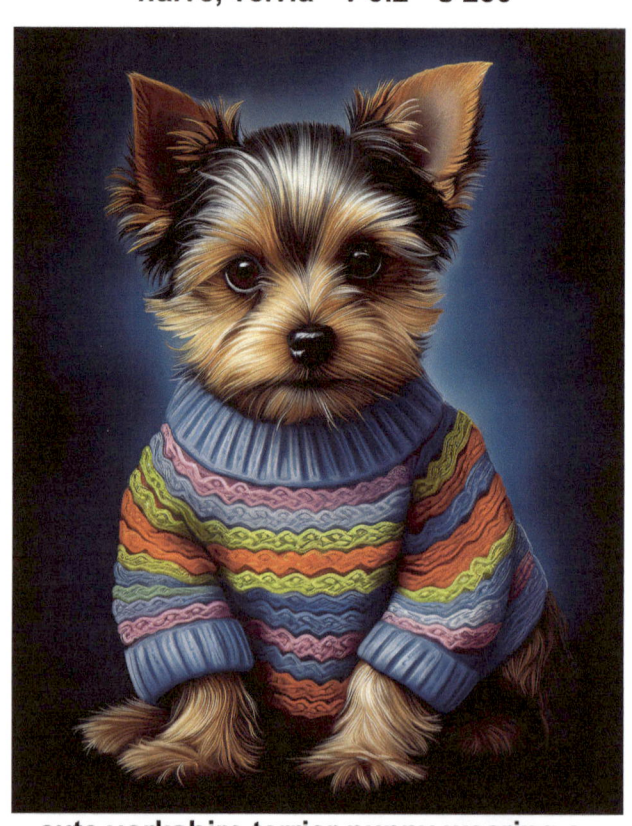

cute yorkshire terrier puppy wearing a knitted sweater, pastel art --v 5.2 --ar 4:5

style of Henri Matisse,
golden retriever dog
--v 5.2 --s 250

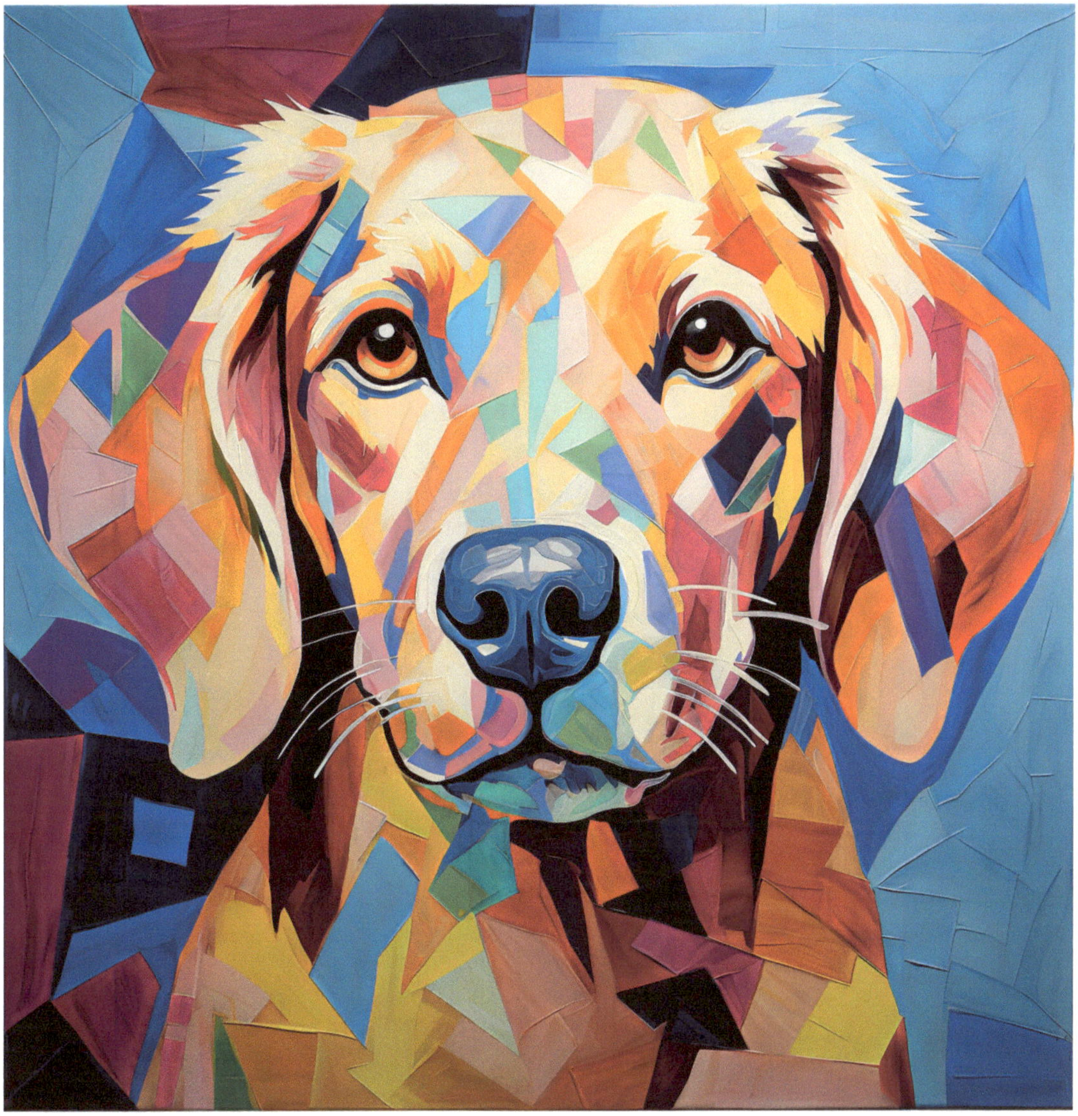

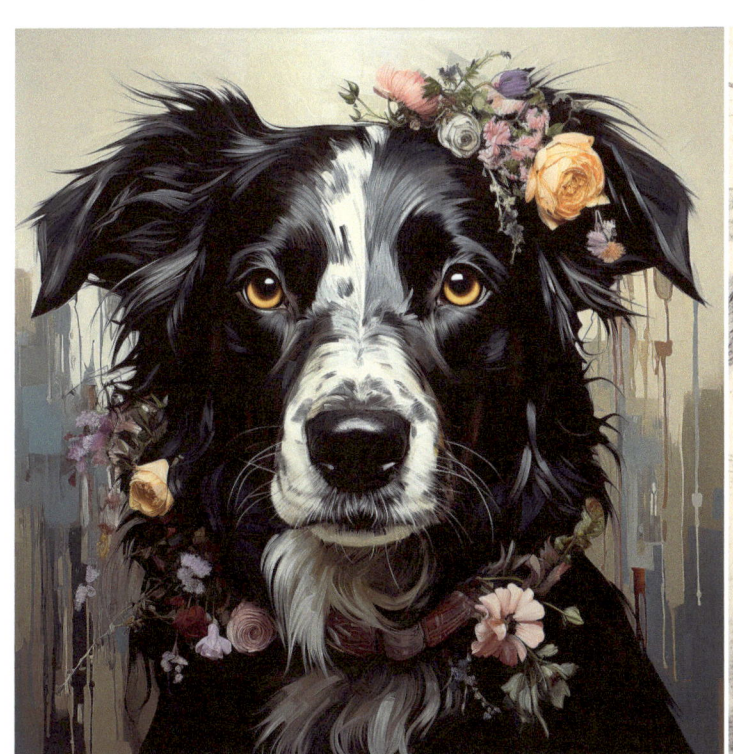

a black dog, wearing a floral crown, playful,
whimsical illustrations, expressive faces,
furry art --v 5.285:110 --s 750

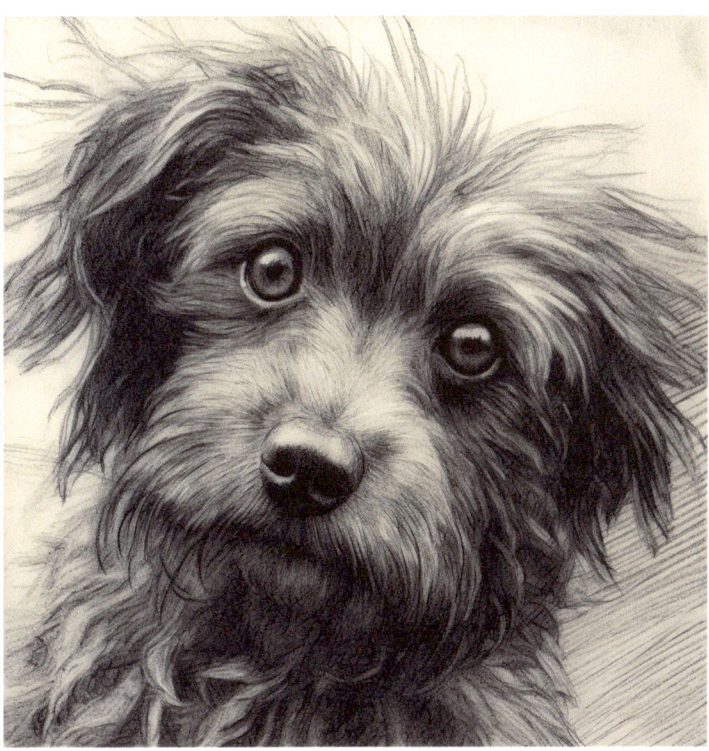

a doodle in drypoint of a labradoodle dog
--v 5.1 --s 250

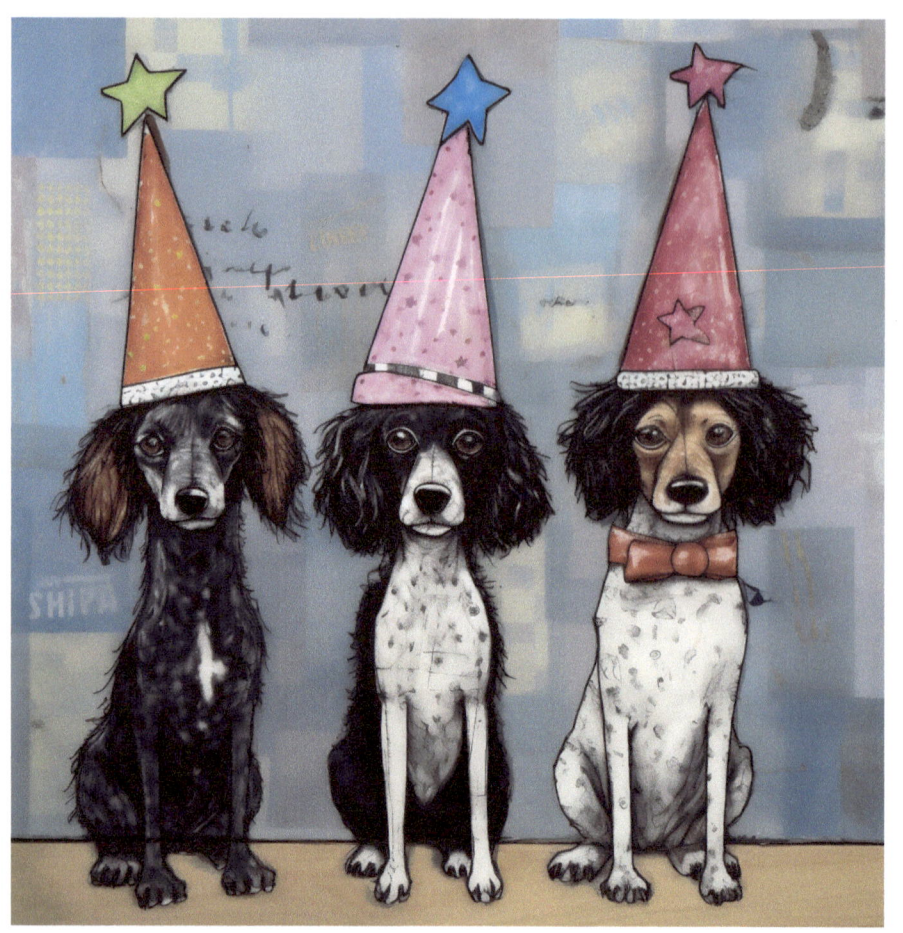

a row of cute miniature silly quirky dogs wearing funny hats, a collage of mixed media art made with tissue paper, maga- zine and newspaper clippings, oil paint, graphite pencil lines and fabric --v 5.2 --weird 50

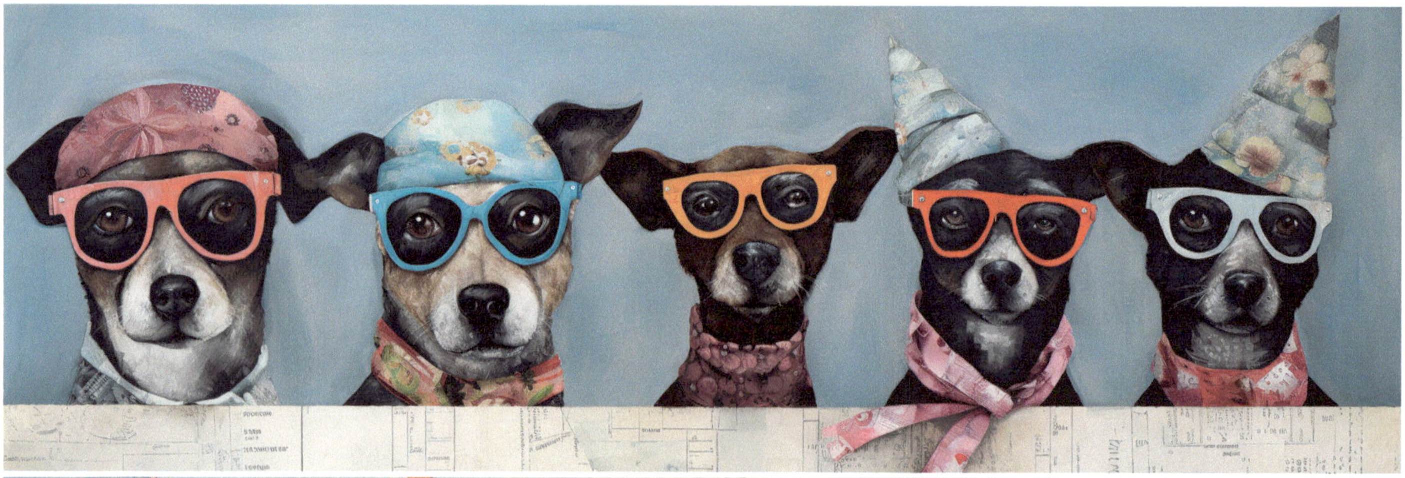

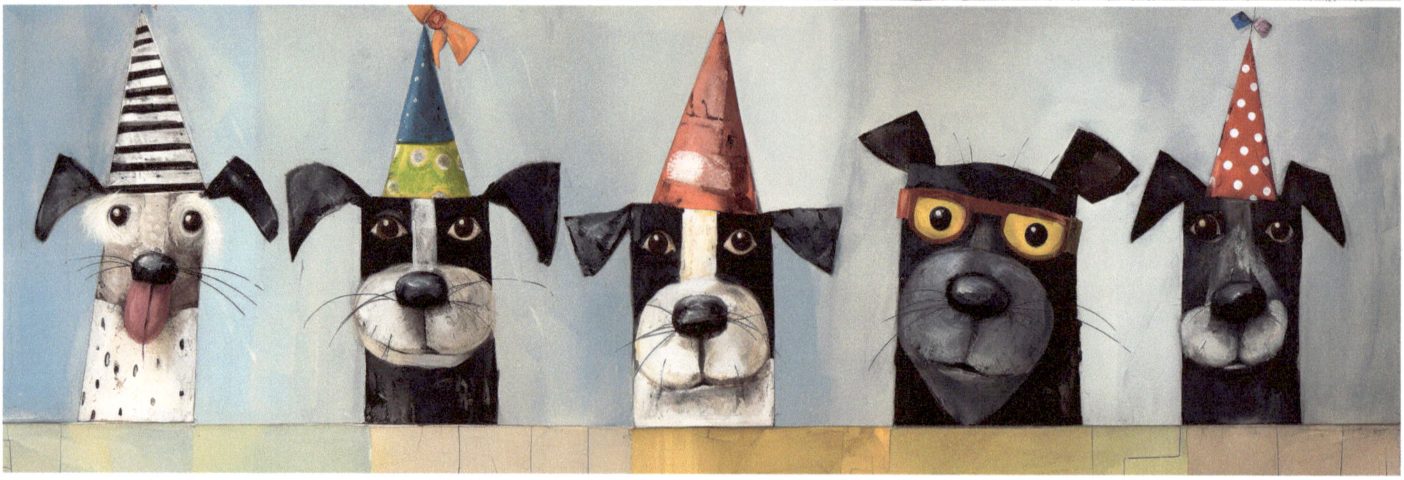

a row of cute miniature silly quirky dogs wearing funny hats, a collage of mixed media art made with tissue paper, magazine and newspaper clippings, oil paint, graphite pencil lines and fabric, in the style of playful surrealism, whimsical --v 5.2 --ar 775:250

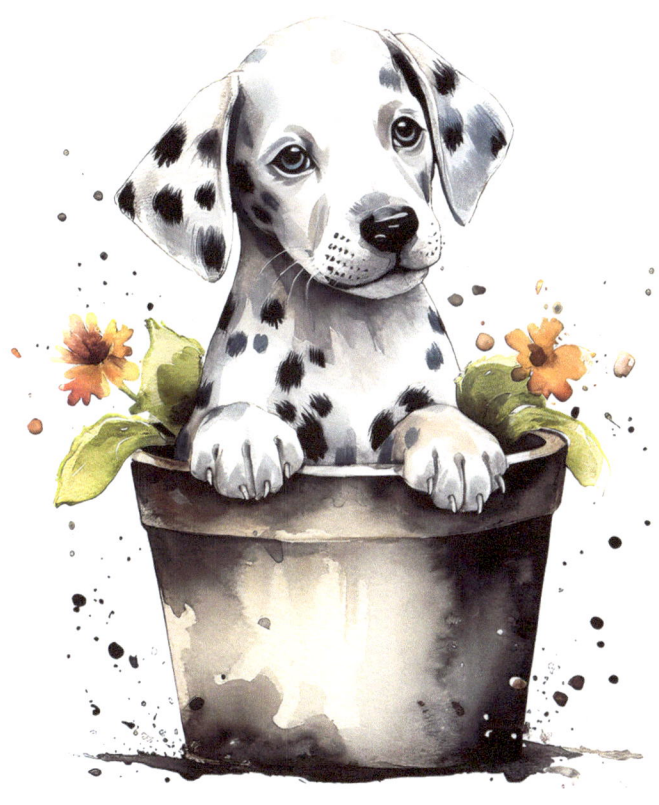

a cute watercolor Dalmatian puppy sitting in a flower pot, white background clipart --v 5.1

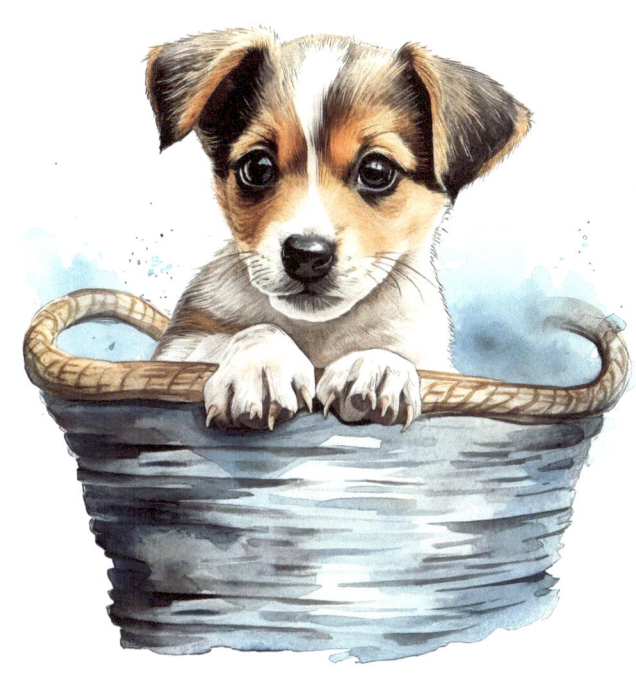

a cute watercolor puppy sitting in a basket, white background clipart --v 5.1

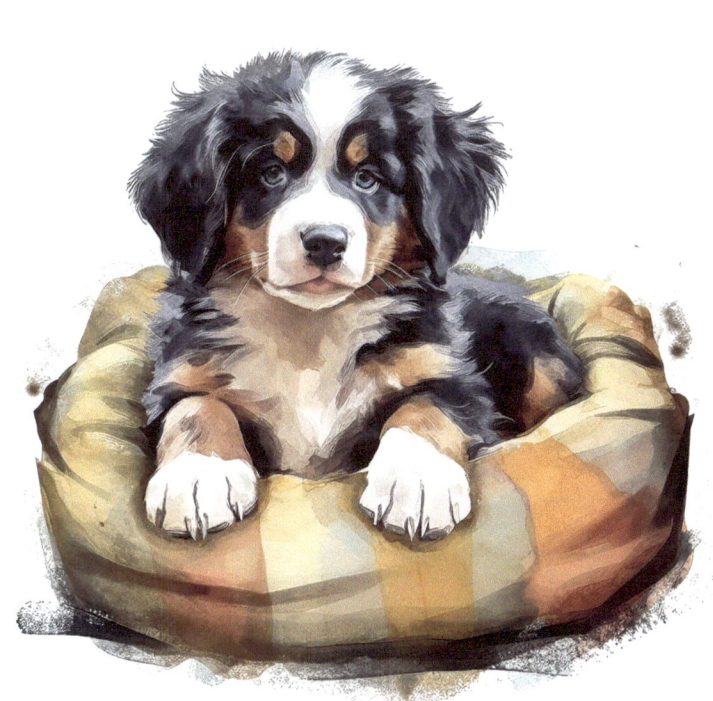

a cute watercolor Bernese puppy sitting on a dog bed, white background clipart --v 5.1

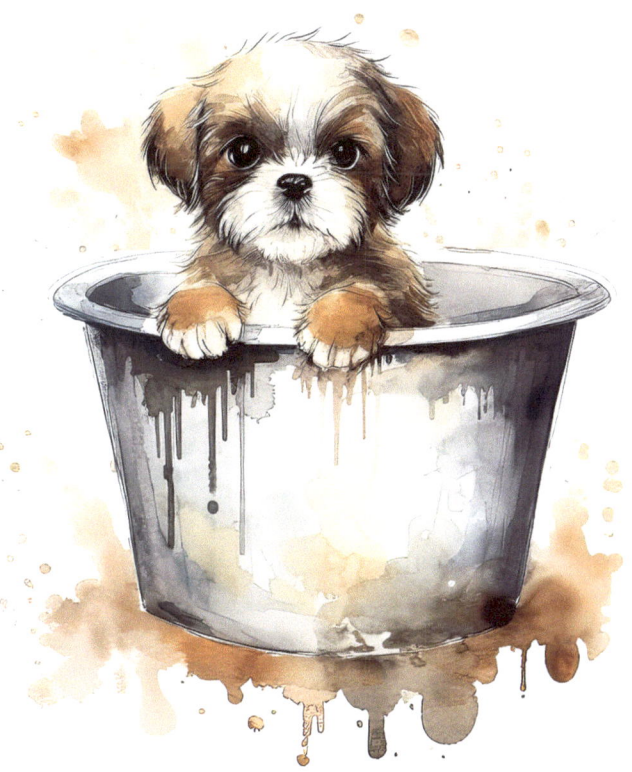

a cute watercolor Shih tzu puppy in a bath, white background clipart --v 5.1

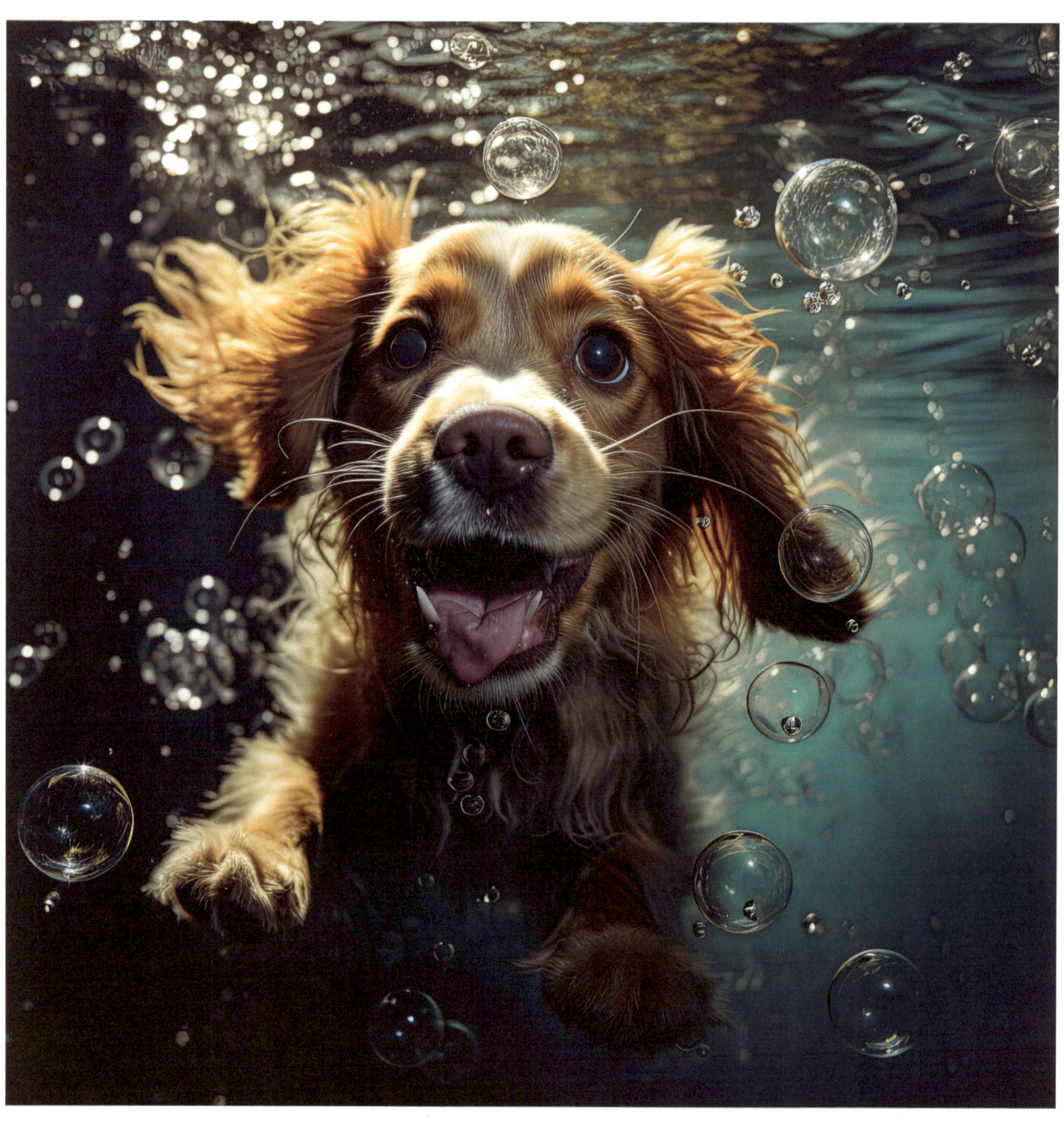

a dog playing with bubbles under the water, in the style of vray tracing, environmental portraiture, smilecore, light amber and emerald, national geographic photo, motion blur panorama, hasselblad 1600f --v 5.2 --s 250

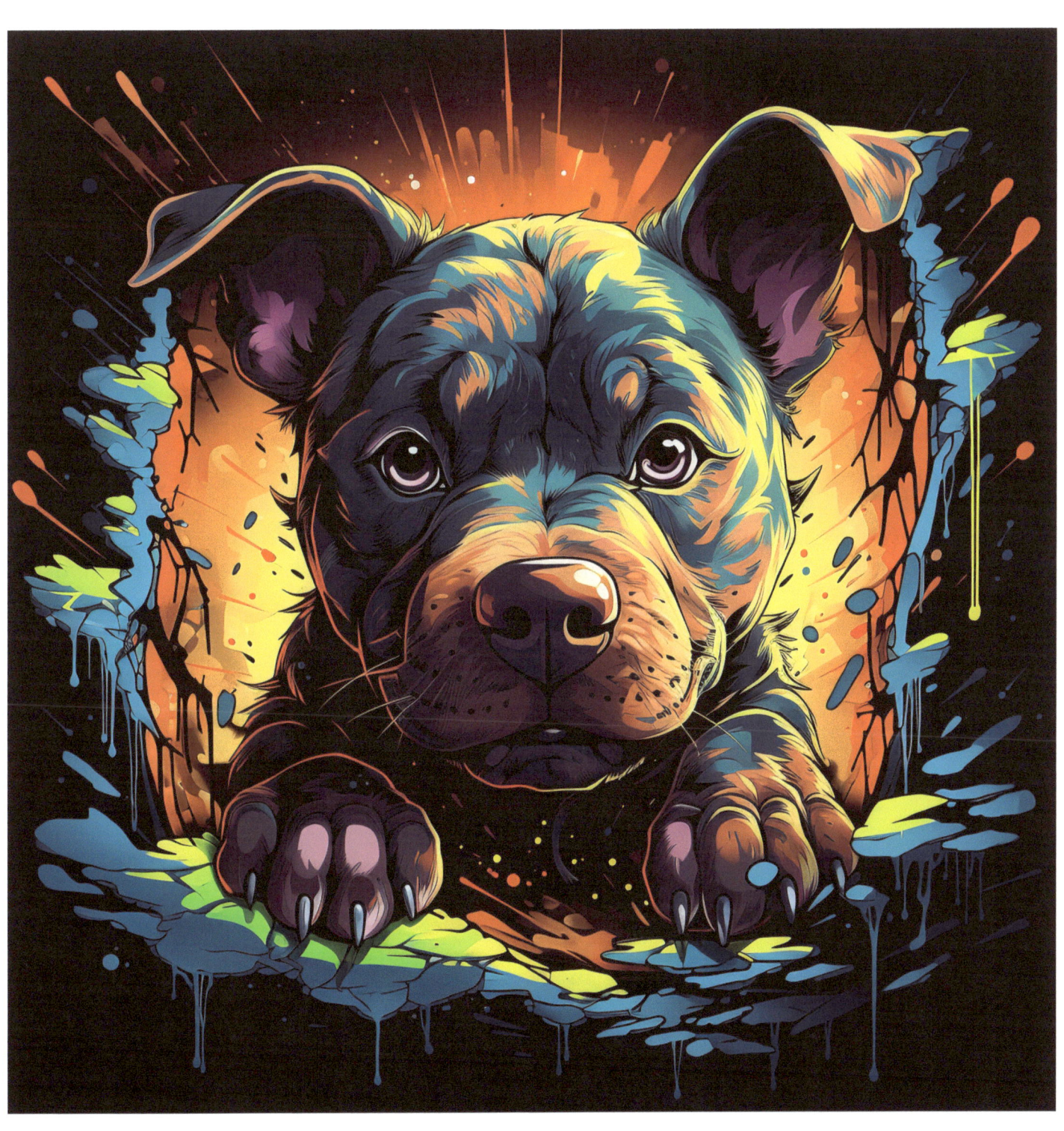

an image of a pitbull puppy jumping out from a hole in a wall, in the style of psychedelic illustration, neon light, splashes of paint, hyper-detailed illustrations, colorful, eye-catching compositions --v 5.2 --s 250

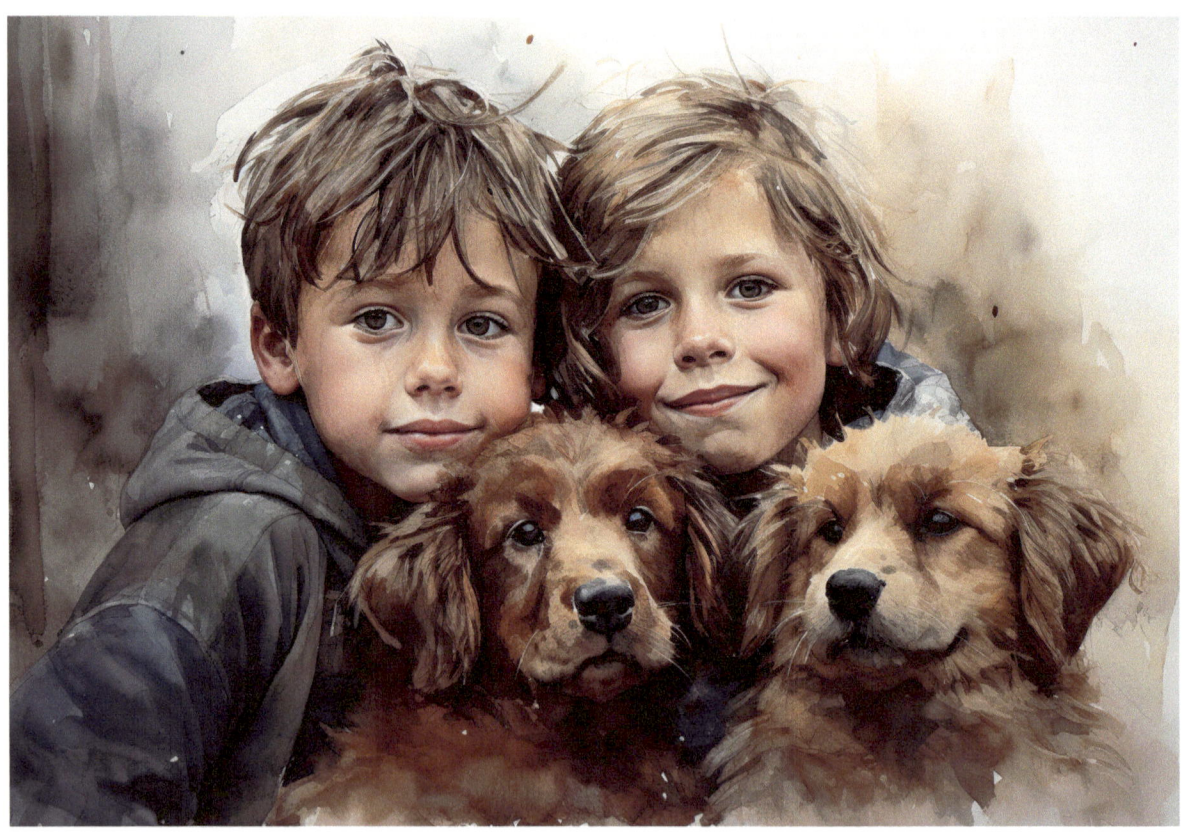

portrait of a little girl on a snowy landscape with dog, in the style of soft gradients, light pink and light bronze, 32k uhd, aquarellist, landscape painter --v 5.2 --ar 128:85 --s 250

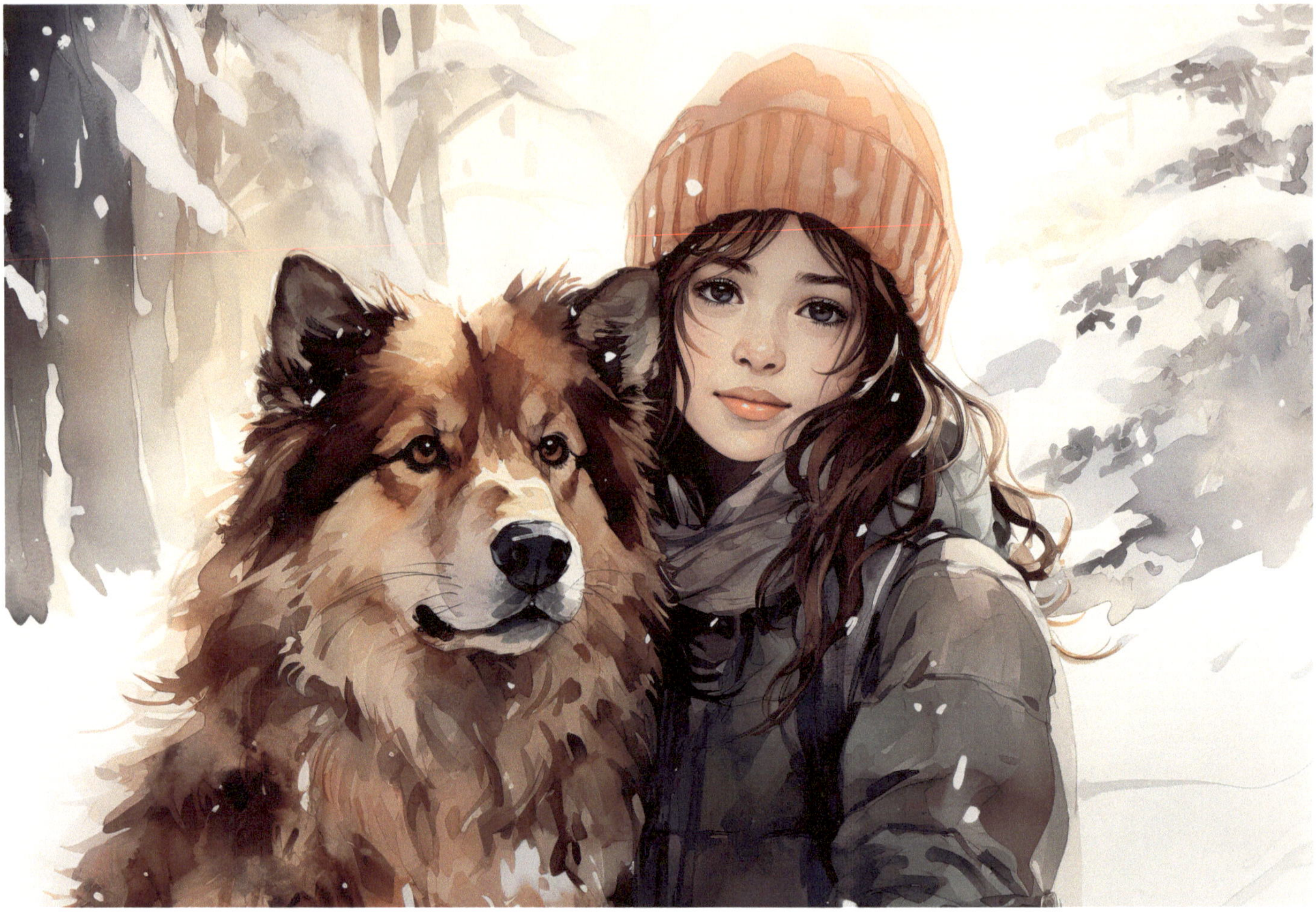

watercolor painting of kids with dogs, in the style of photobashing, cold and detached atmosphere --v 5.2 --ar 128:85 --s 250 a painting in sanyu style, dog, in the style of red and indigo, black and white art, maranao art, young british artists, folk art inspiration, post-impressionist printmaker --v 5.2 --s 250

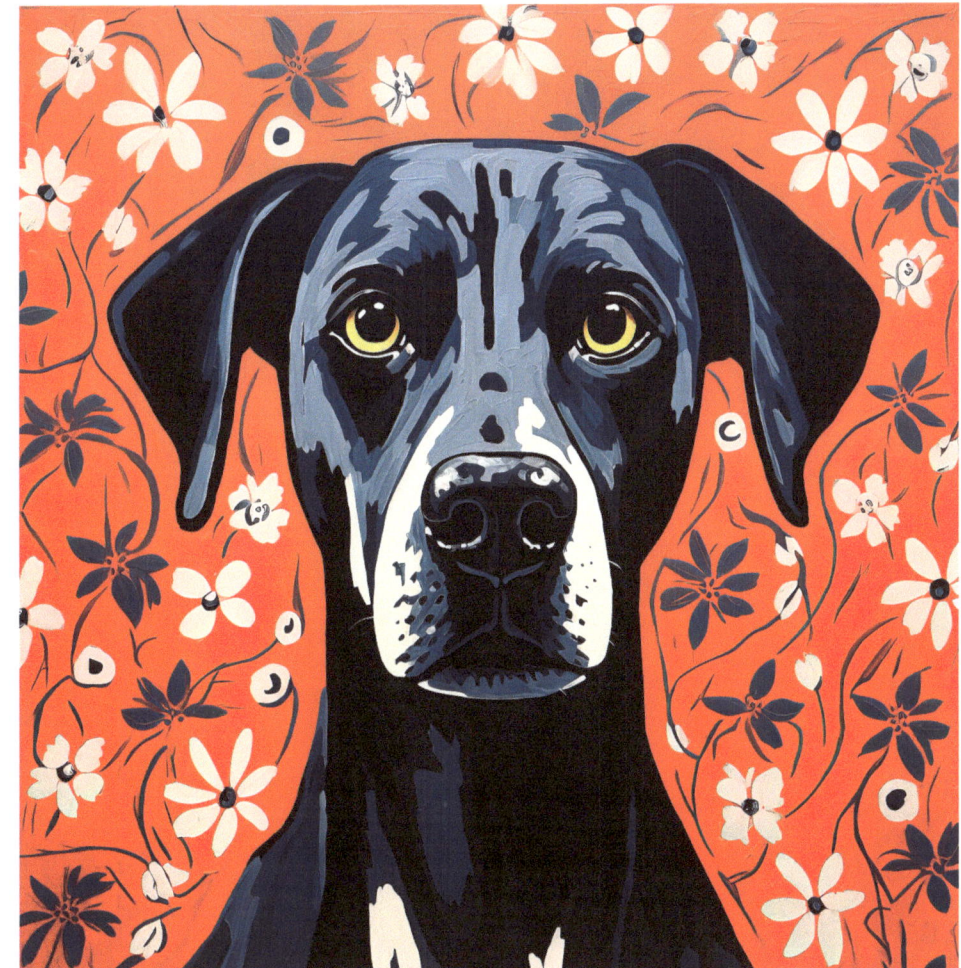

a drawing of a white dog with black hair, in the style of dark yellow and red, pop art, intaglio printmaking, blink-and-you-miss-it detail, dark orange and white, comic strip art, ceramic tapestries --v 5.2 --s 250

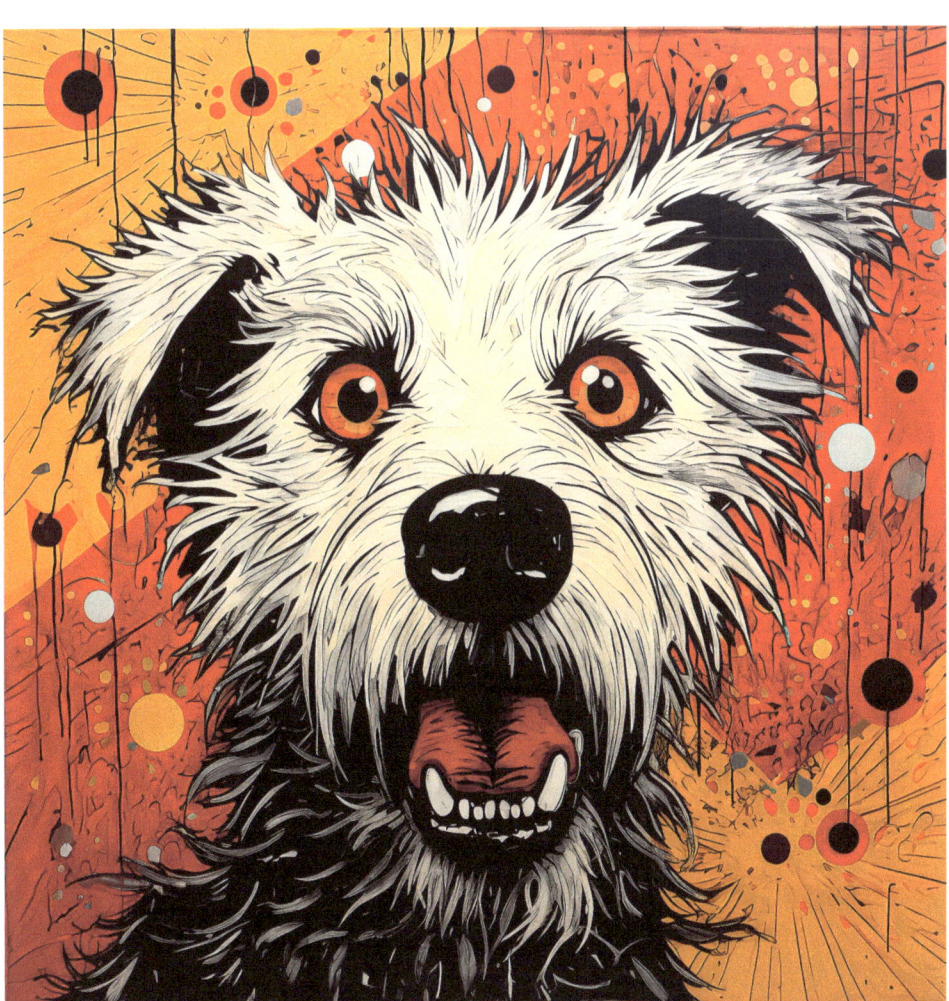

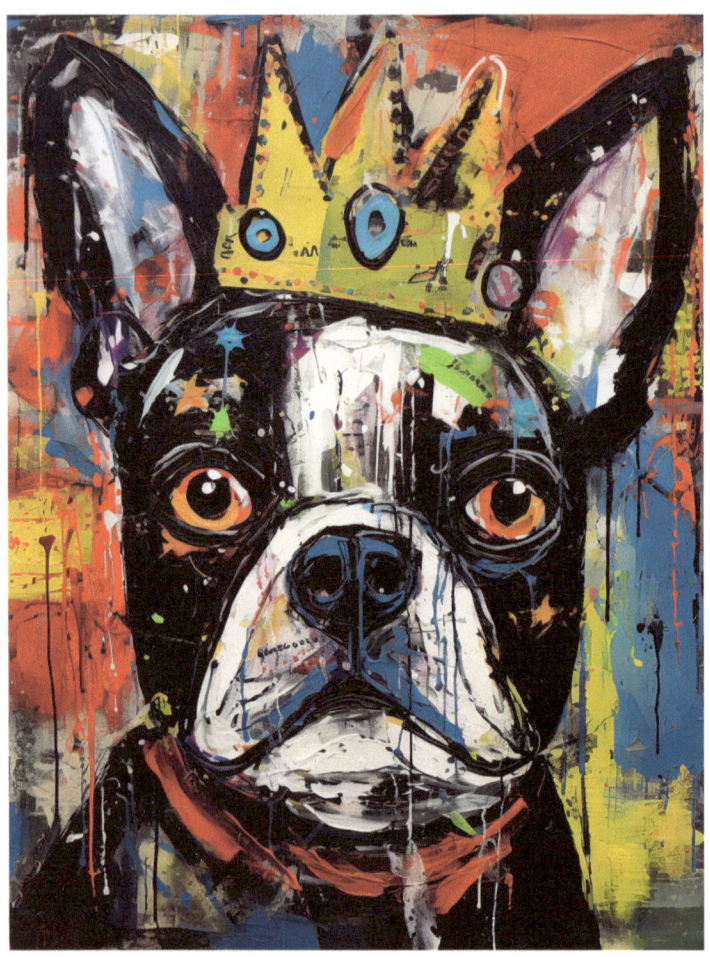

portrait of a dog with a crown in the style of jean-michel basquiat --v 5.2 --ar 85:110

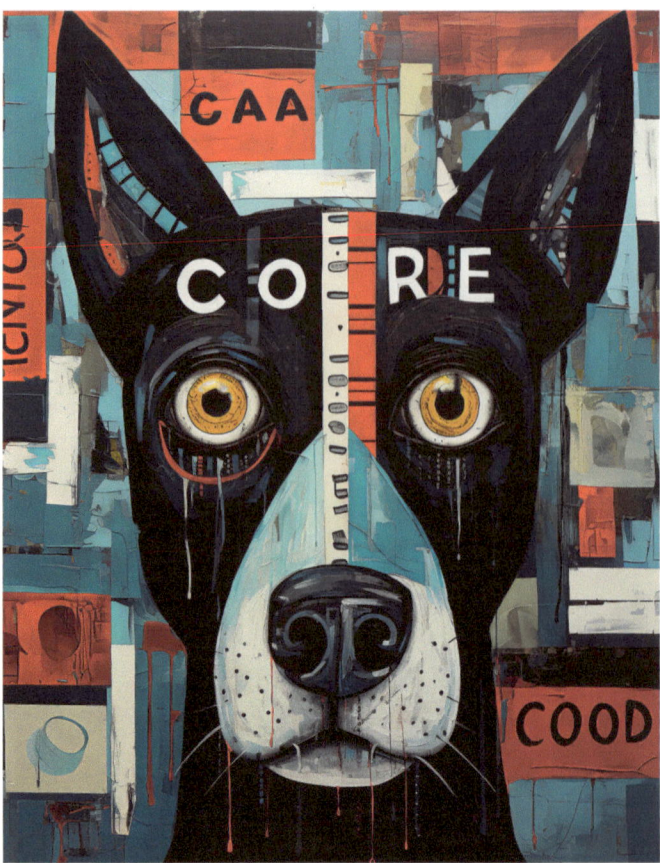

style of contemporary canadian art, caninecore, flat perspective, dark cyan and red, black and white imagery, inventive character designs, recycled material murals --v 5.2 --ar 31:39 --s 250

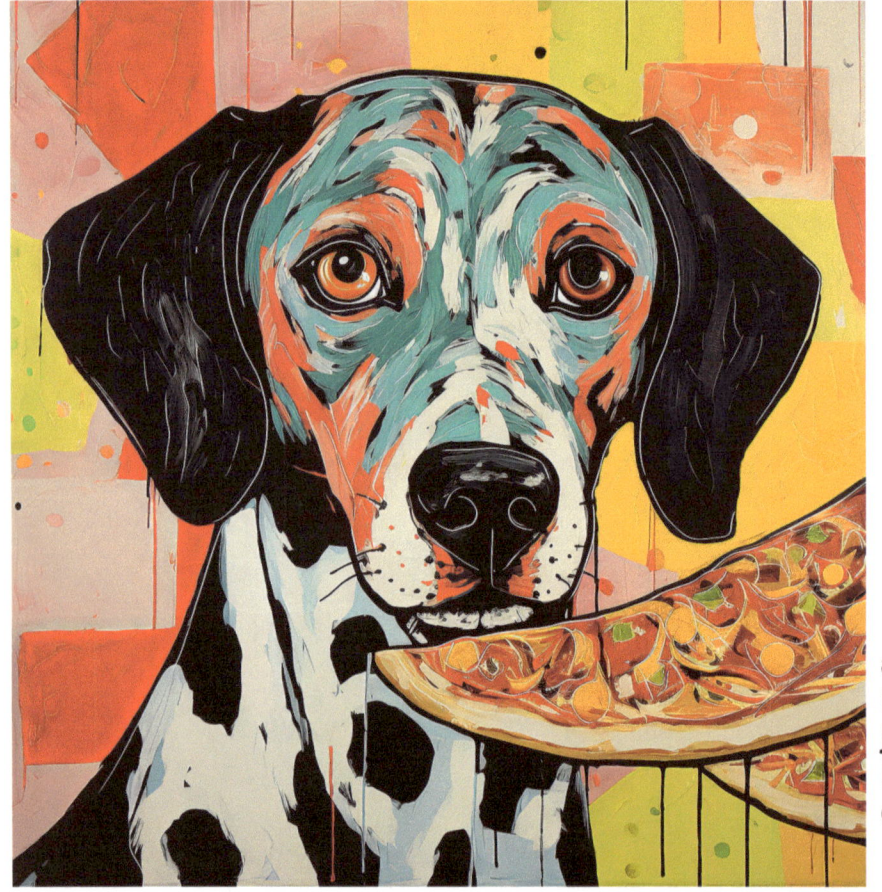

a painting of a dog holding a pizza, in the style of pop art silkscreening, jim lively, light red and yellow, paul henry, close-up, fernand leger, etchings --v 5.1

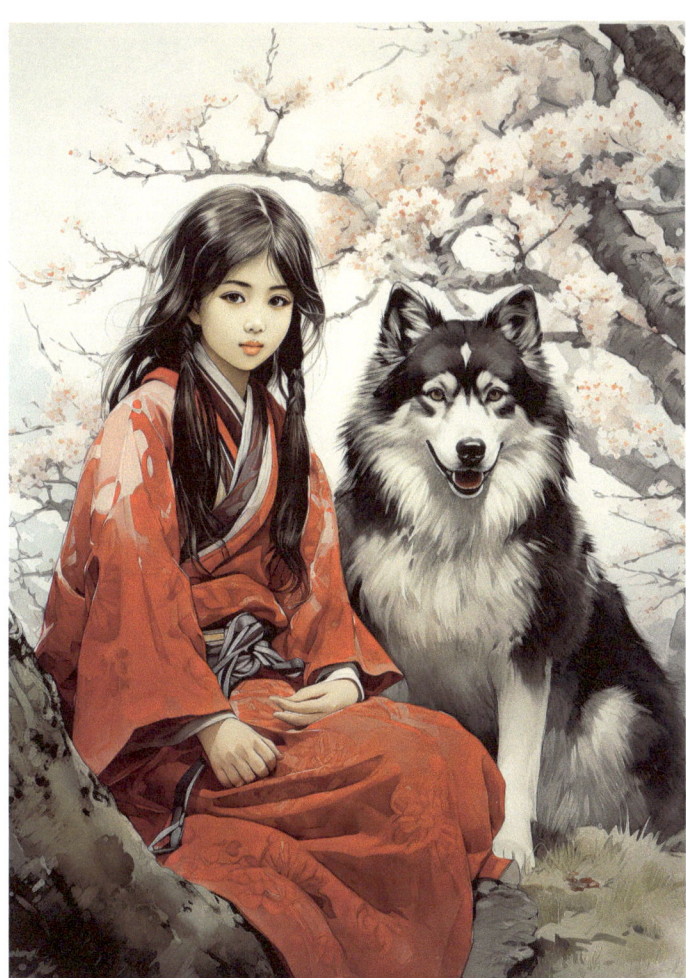
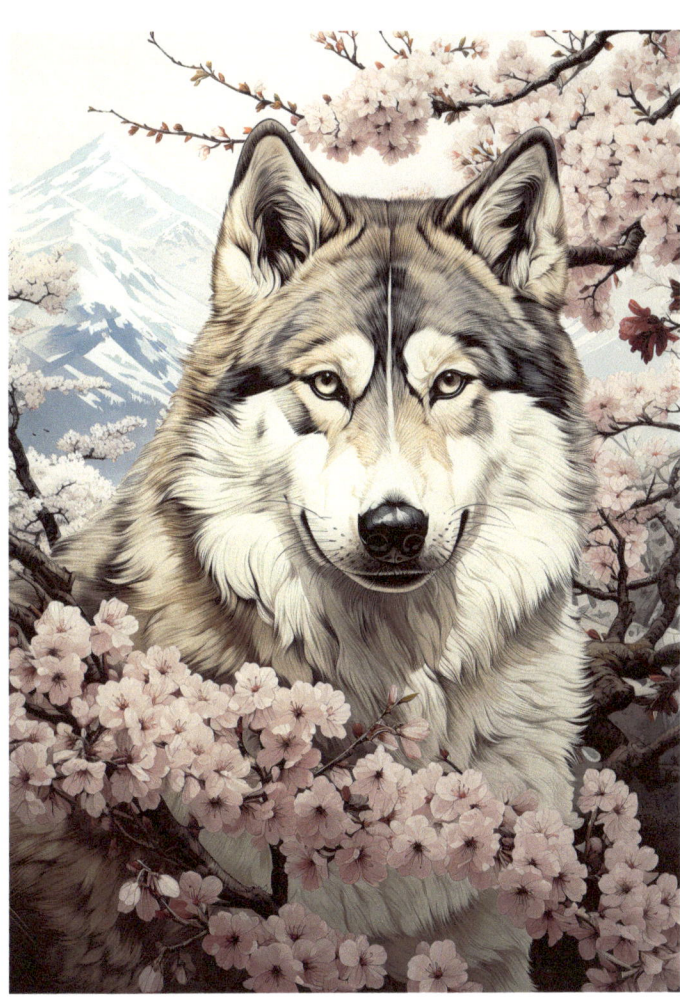

juzu sakura 1905 peking dog art print, in the style of 1860–1969, silver and red, dolly kei, editorial illustrations, intense gaze --v 5.2 --ar 71:98 --s 250

Really cute puppies with flowers, a collage of mixed media art made with tissue paper, magazine and newspaper clippings, oil paint, graphite pencil lines and fabric, in the style of playful surrealism, whimsical --v 5.2 --s 750

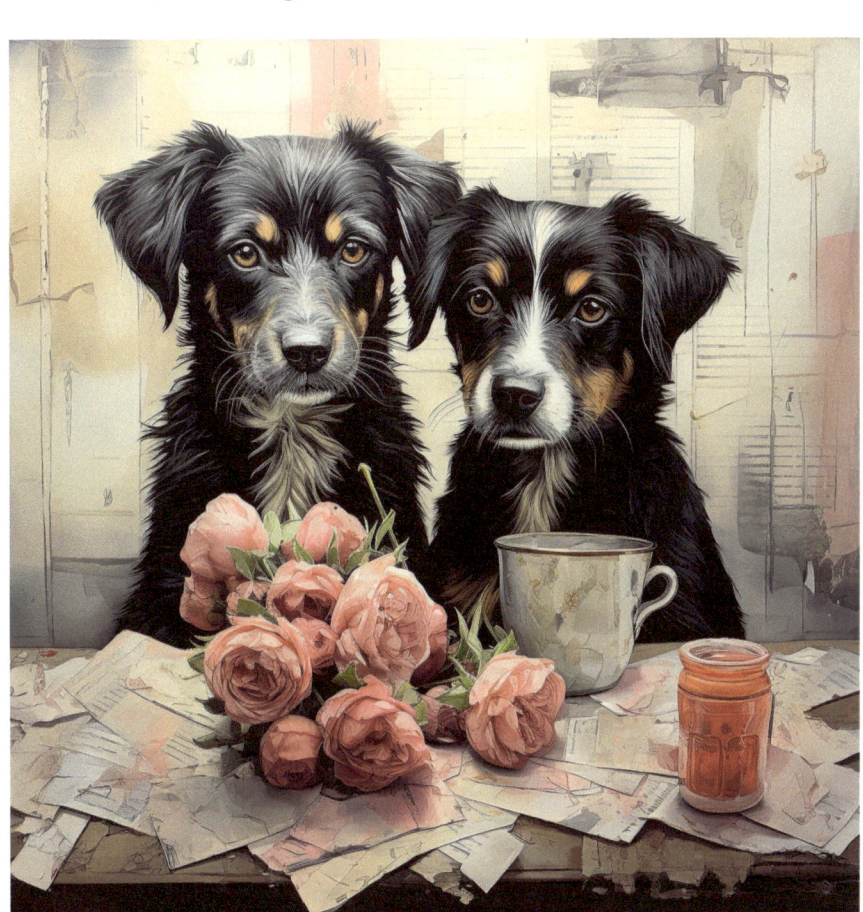

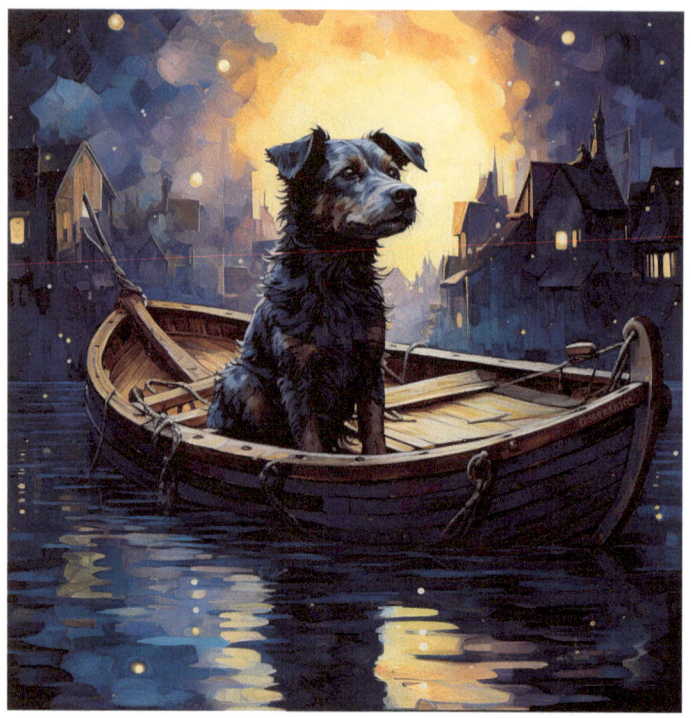

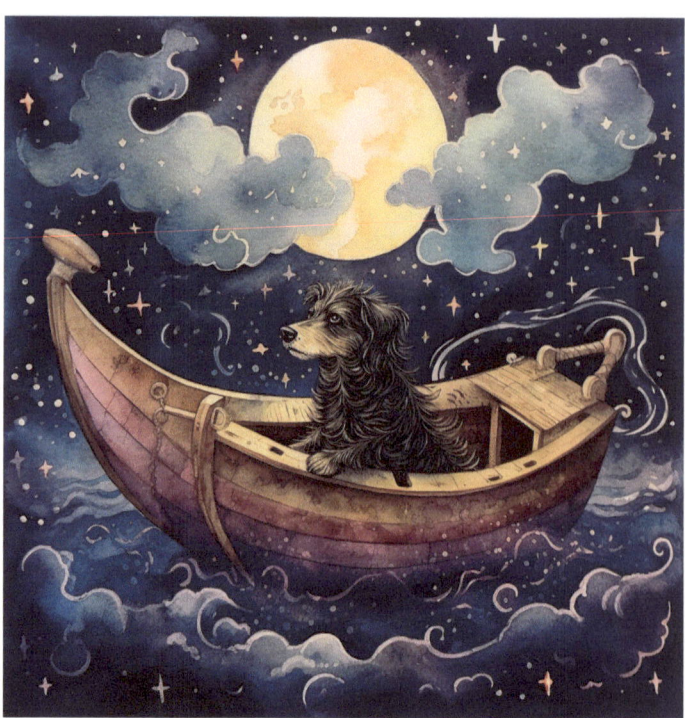

a beautiful painting of a dog in a boat on the water, in the style of luminous skies, calligraphy-inspired, watercolorist, dark purple and yellow, found object inspired happenings, whimsical --v 5.2 --s 250

Same prompt using --v 5.1

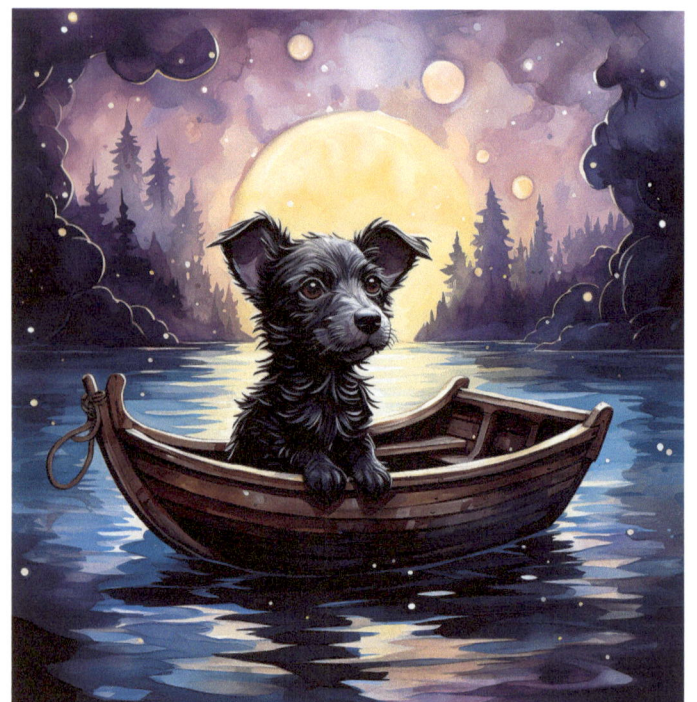

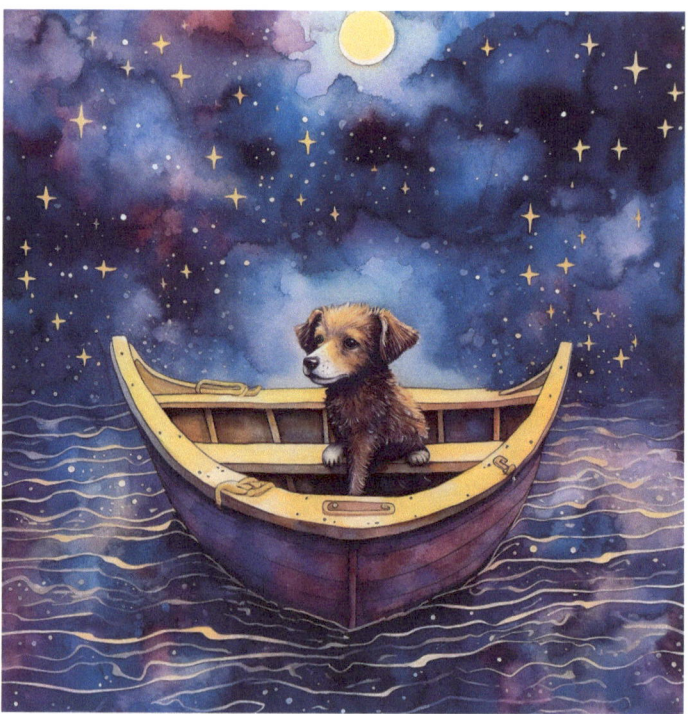

a beautiful painting of a small puppy in a boat on the water, in the style of luminous skies, calligraphy-inspired, watercolorist, dark purple and yellow, found object inspired happenings, whimsical --v 5.2 --s 250

Same prompt using --v 5.1

style of Monet,
cute dachshund puppy
--v 5.2 --s 250

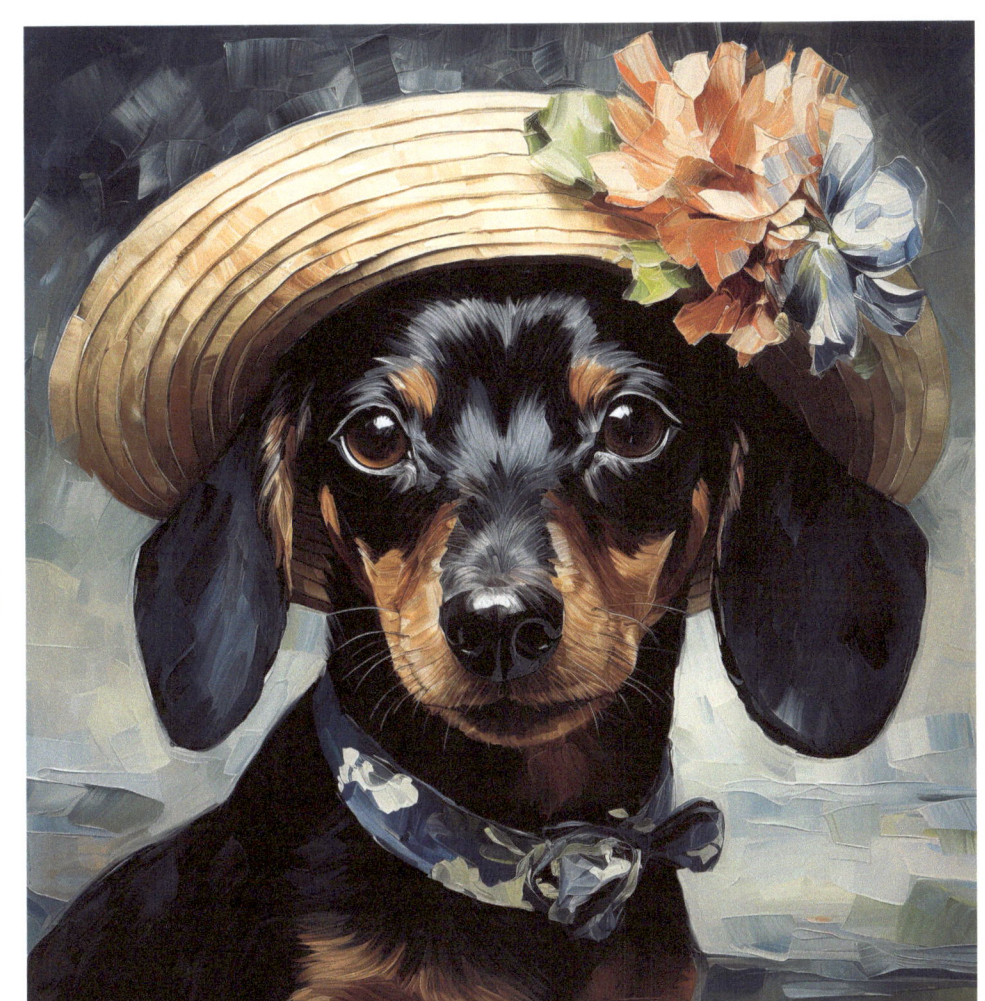

style of Egon Schiele,
bernese mountain dog
--v 5.2 --s 250

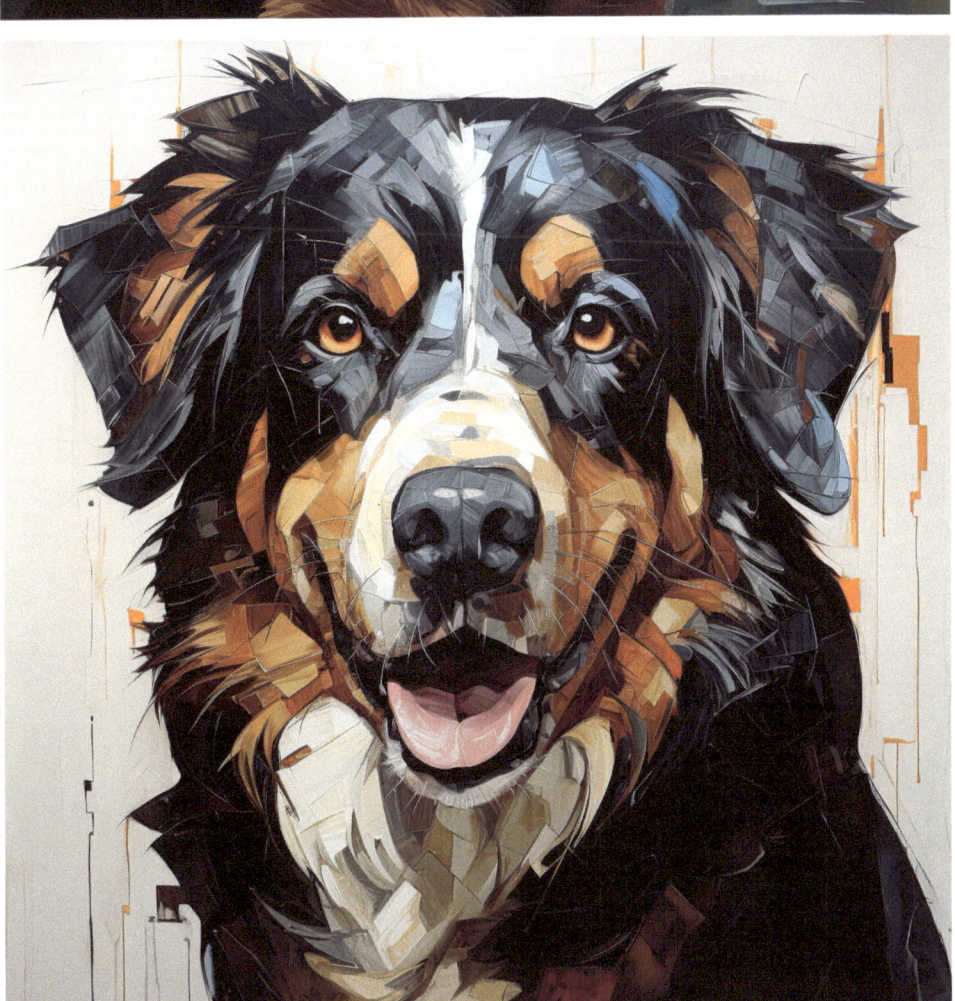

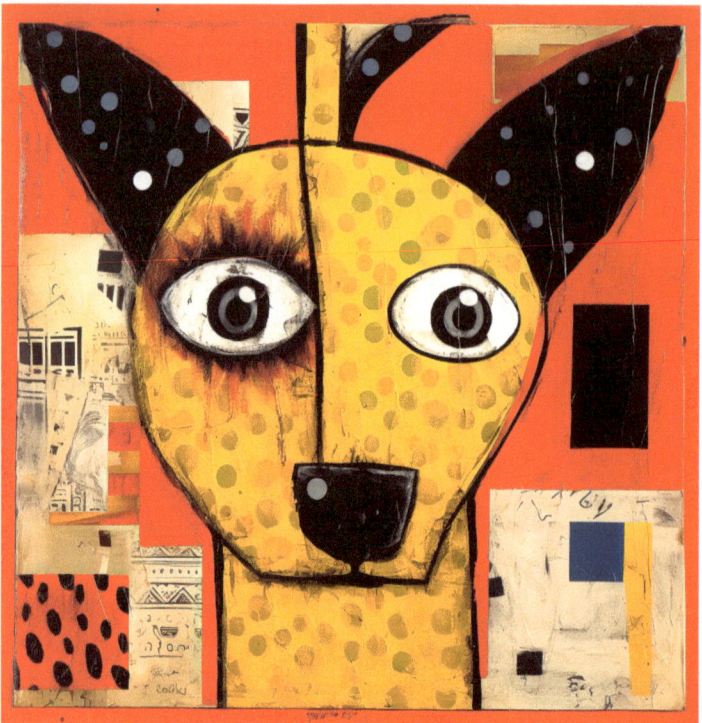

a cartoon dog on a tile has black ears and red eyes, in the style of peter max, dark yellow and white, monotype/monoprint, dark red and light gray, gentle expressions --v 5.1

dalmatian with polka dots on wood, in the style of chromatic experimentation, gray, naive art, multi-coloured minimalism, intaglio, light gray, tactile canvases --v 5.1

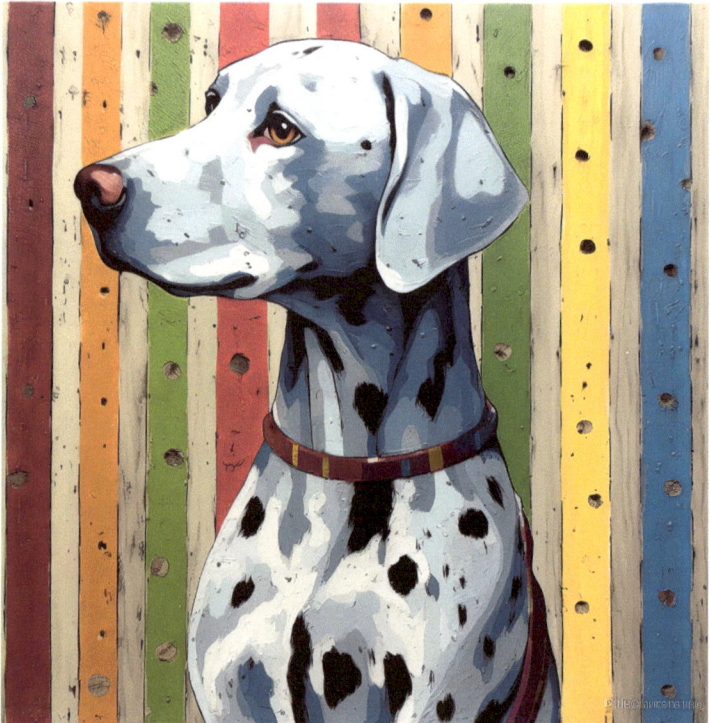

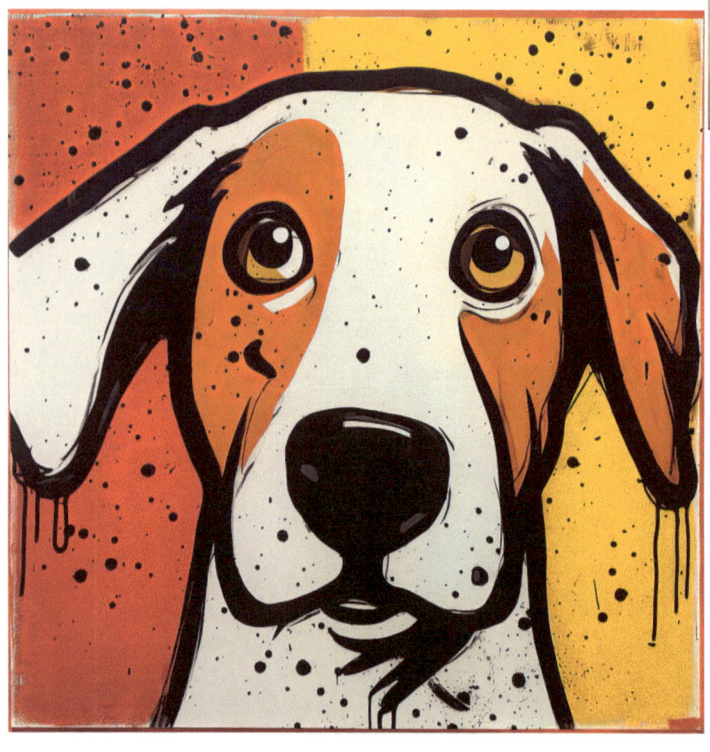

the faces of a brown dog with a yellow shirt, in the style of pop art silkscreening, light red and white, ceramic, cartoonish innocence, rollei prego 90, light white and dark orange, happy expressionism --v 5.1

a shiba inu dog, in the style of ukiyo-e influence, light red and light beige, wilhelmina weber furlong, lithograph --v 5.2

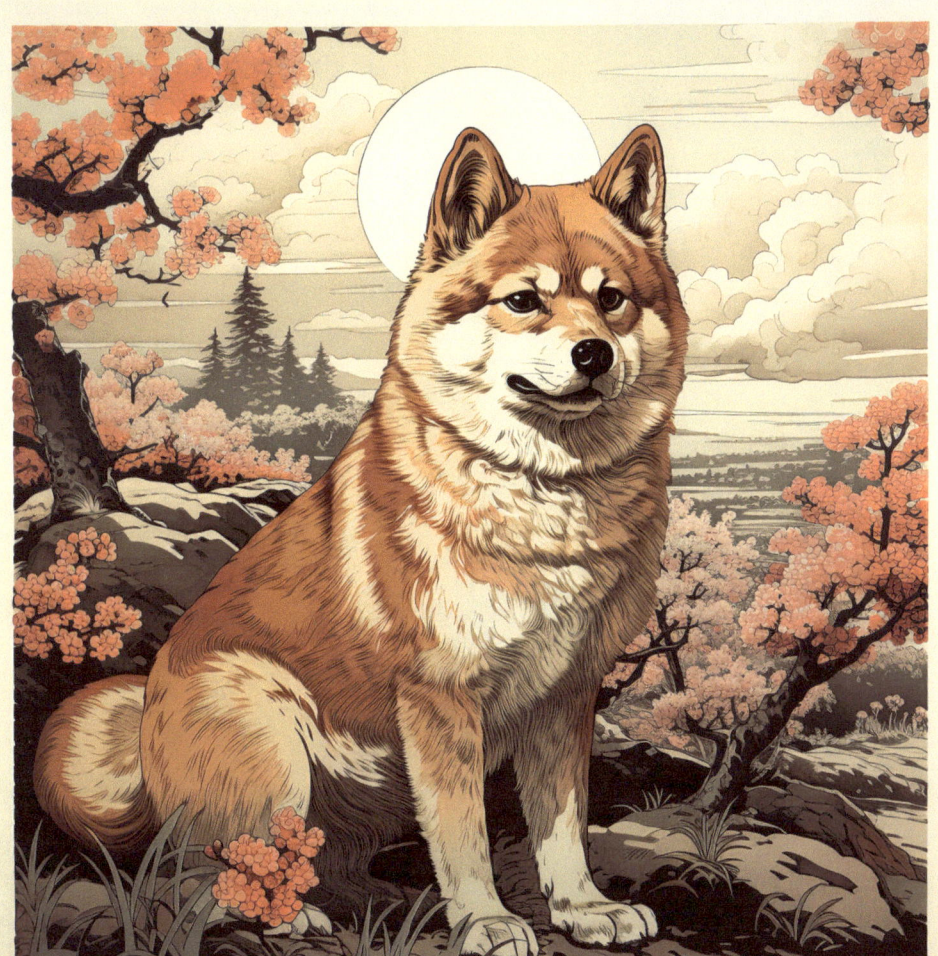

a pekinese dog sitting near a bird cage, in the style of ukiyo-e influence, light red and light beige, chuah thean teng, lithograph, historical illustrations --v 5.2

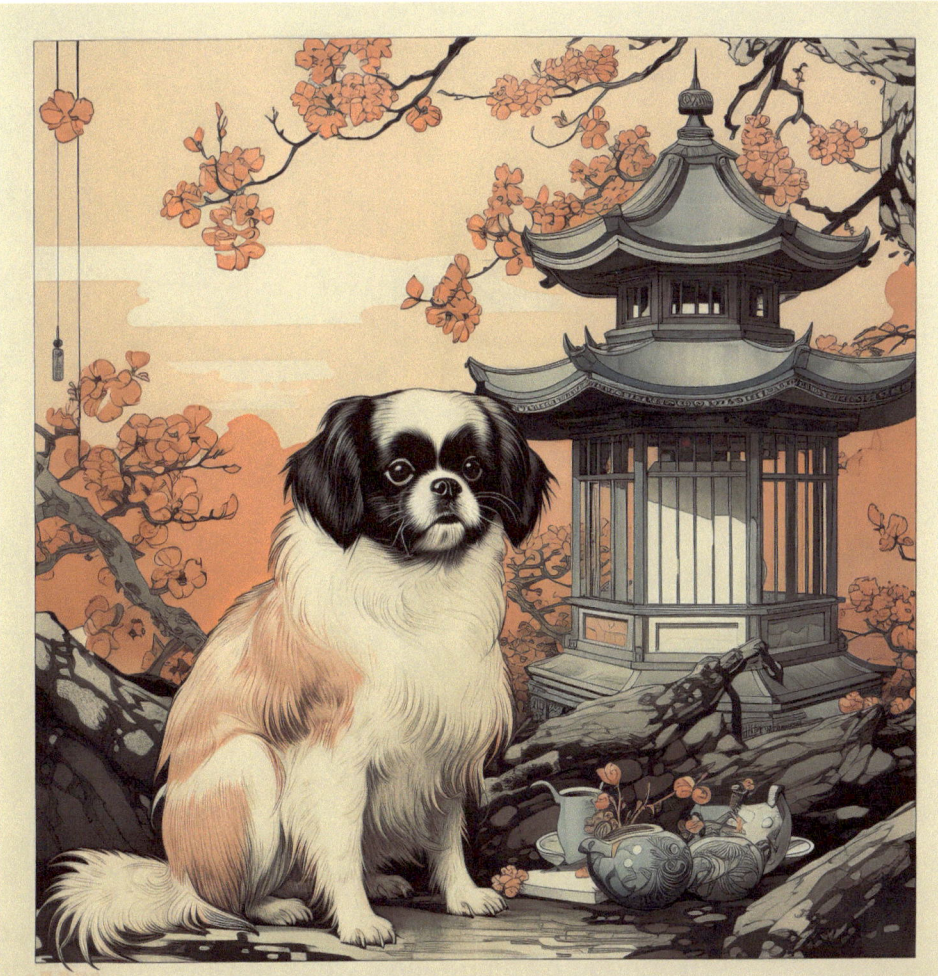

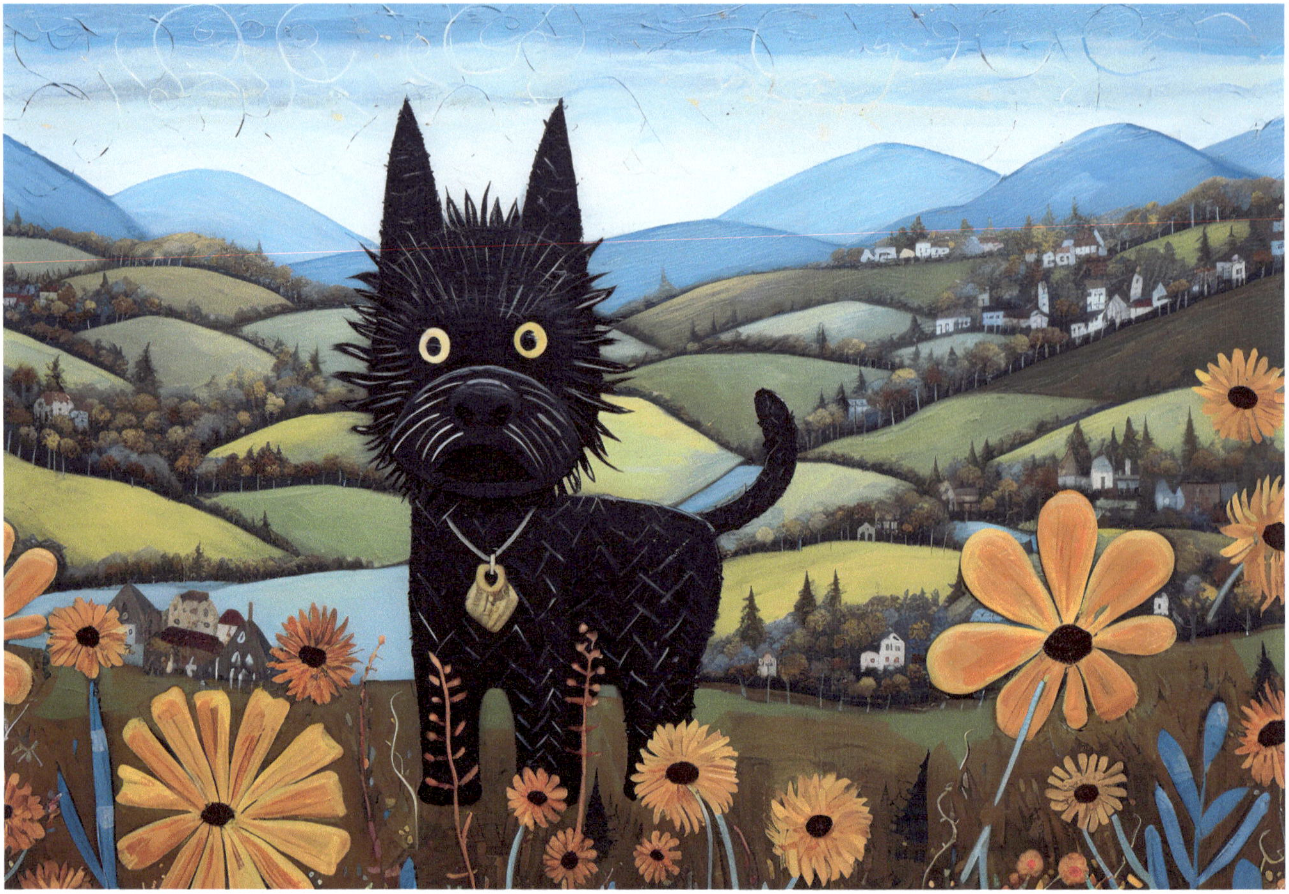

a cute black scottie dog on top of a mountain in Scotland in the style of whimsical folk art, textural landscapes, fawncore, characterful animal portraits, flower power --v 5.1 --ar 12:8

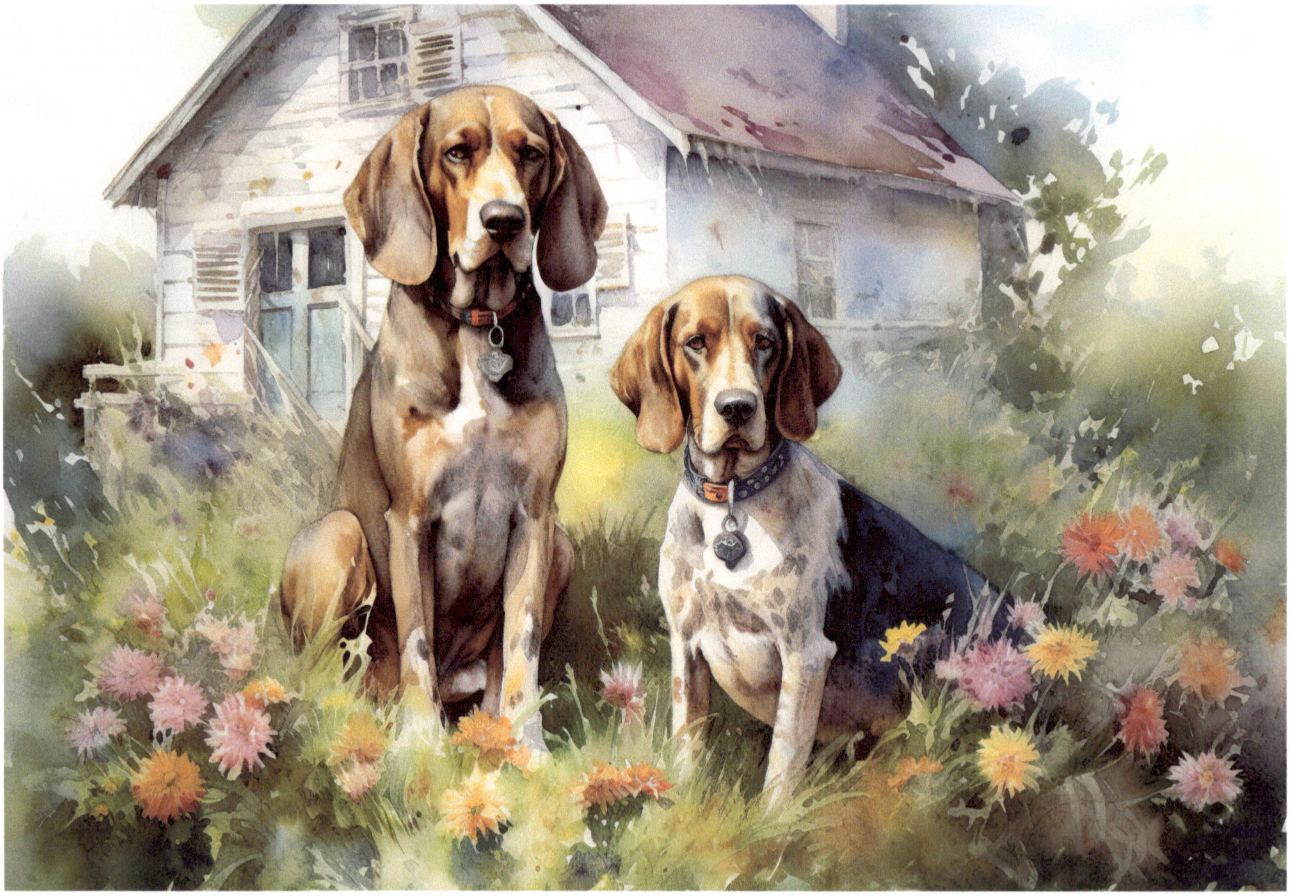

a watercolor painting of A pair of american coonhounds sitting outside a charming cottage, surrounded by blooming garden flowers, cottagecore --v 5.1 --ar 3:2

style of Lautrec, scene of a Bulldog with a classy monocle, walking with purpose in Paris --v 5.2

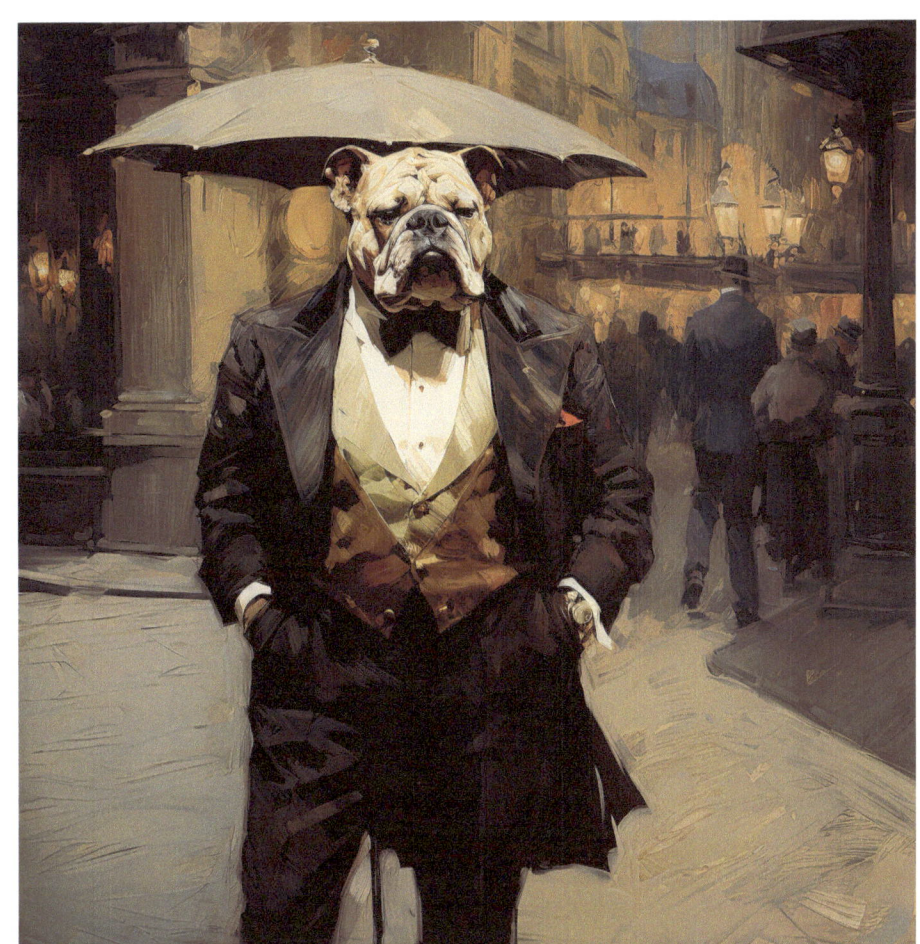

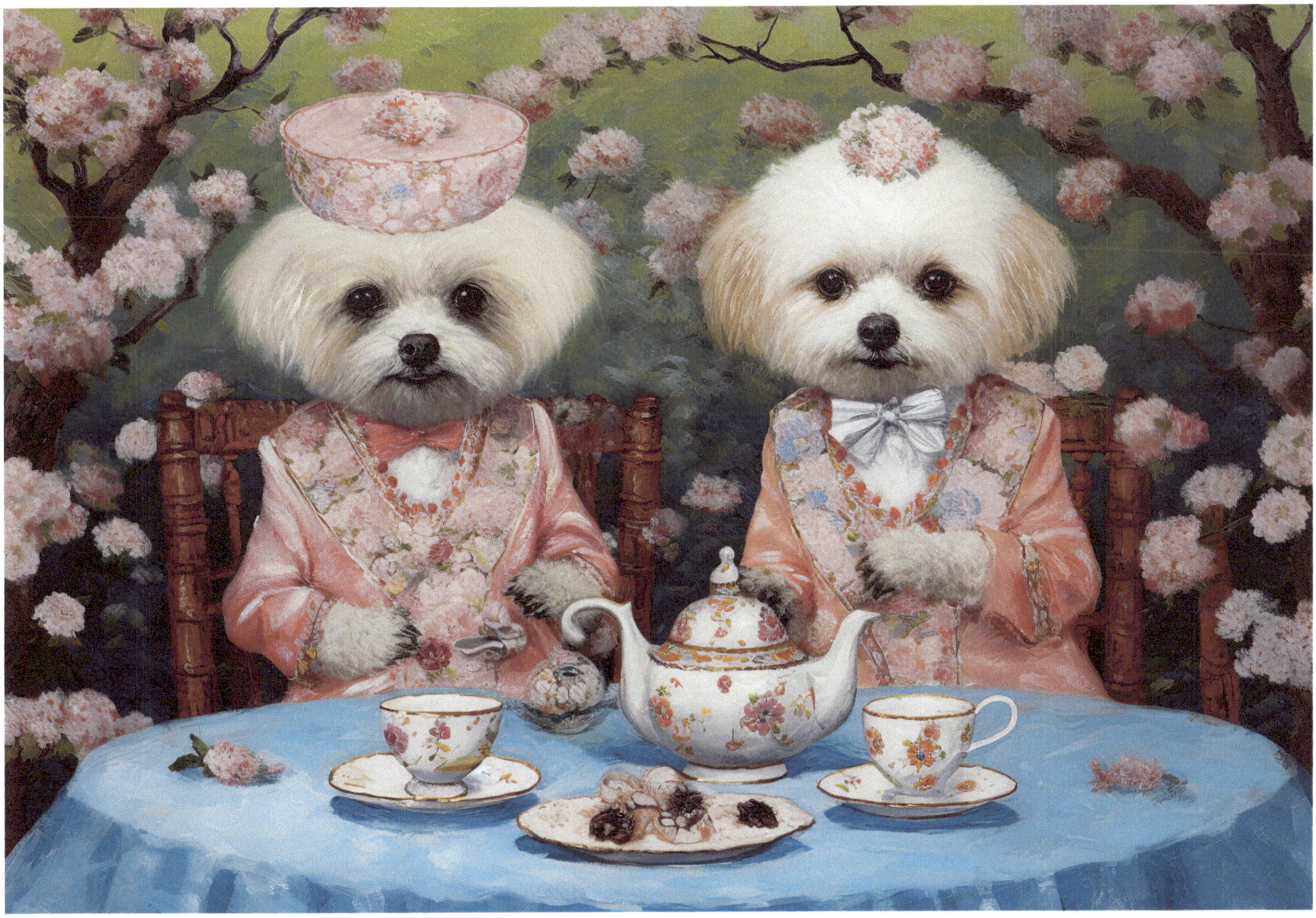

oil painting in the style of matisse of two maltese terrier dogs wearing Victorian attire, seated around a whimsical tea party set in a blossoming garden --v 5.1 --s 380 --ar 3:2

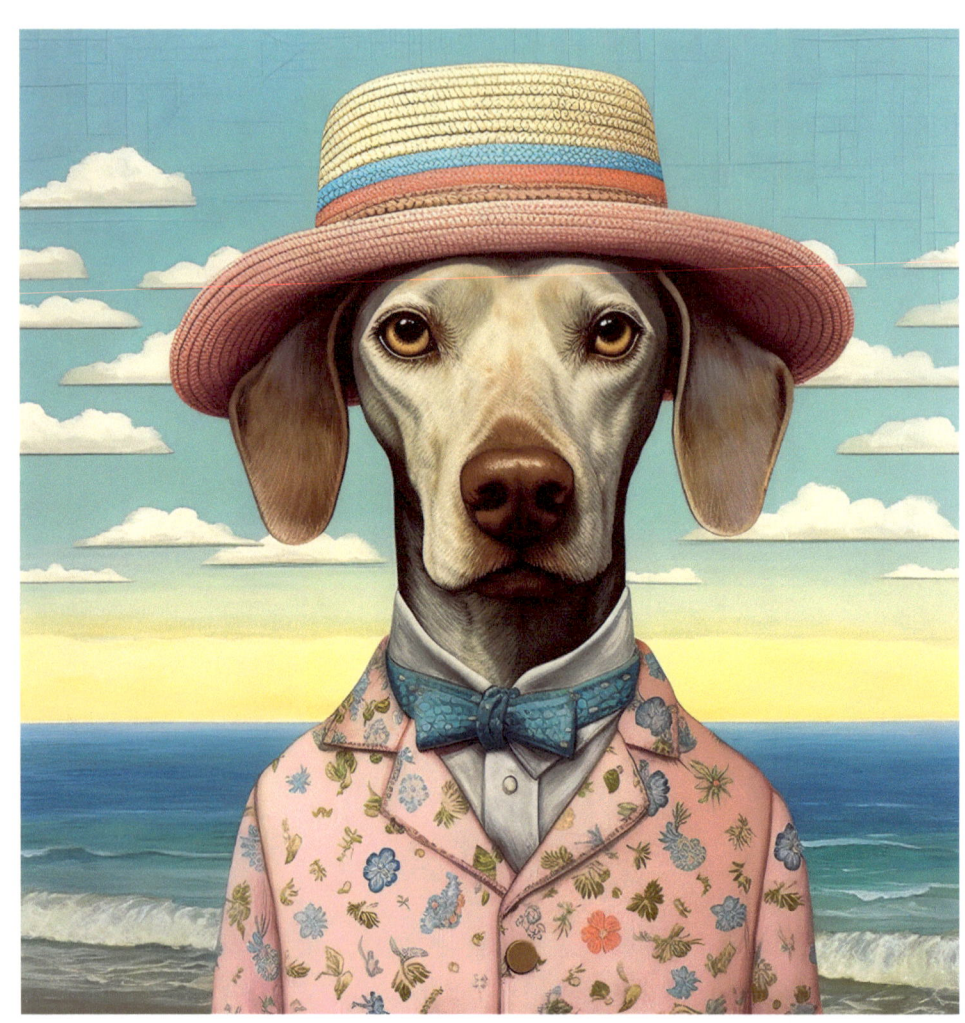

dog wearing pink and pink colors, in the style of contemporary folk art, light brown and sky-blue, beach portraits, layered fabrications, fanciful illustrations --v 5.1

a painting of a white dog with dots on the face, in the style of light indigo and light green, love and romance, figuratively textured, debbie criswell, helene schjerfbeck, jane crowther --v 5.1

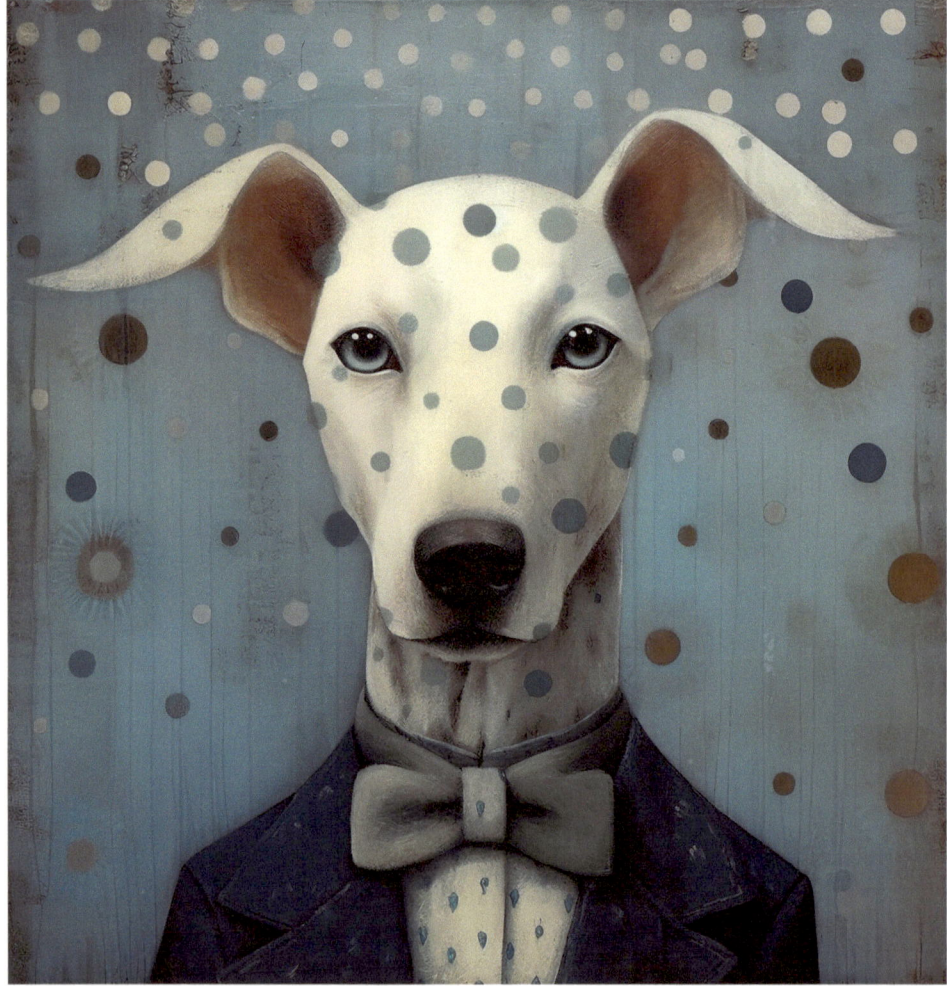

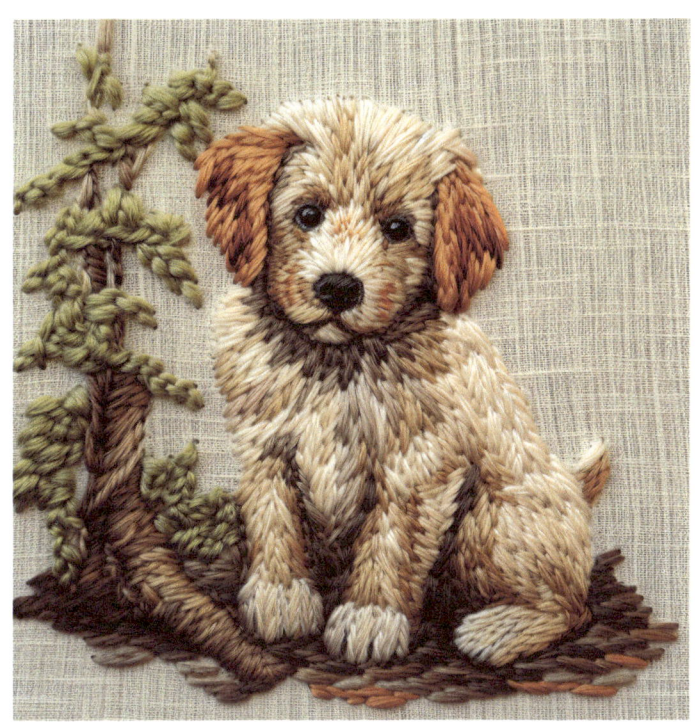

a cute puppy picture in
stumpwork embroidery
--v 5.1

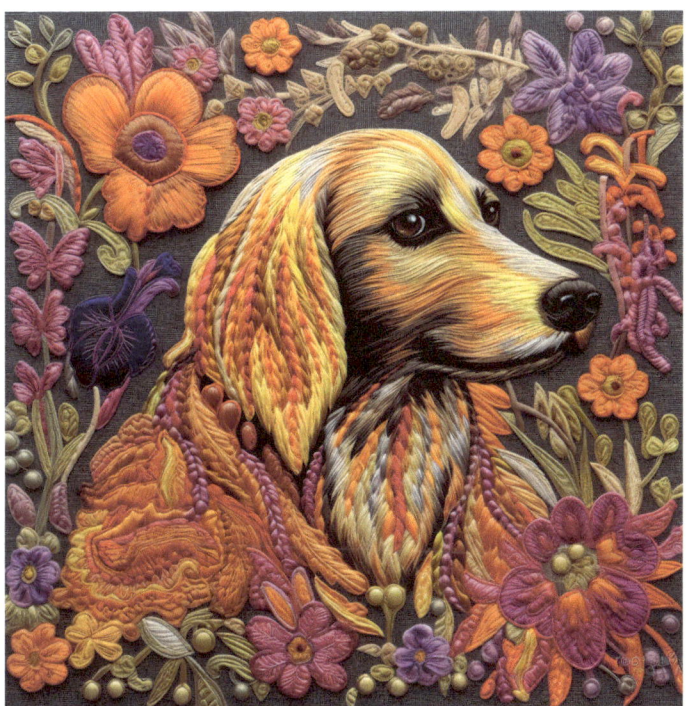

embroidery artwork embroidered
dog and flower designs, in the
style of colorful woodcarvings,
light gray and magenta, made of
flowers, light yellow and light
orange, illustration, majestic
composition, accurate and
detailed --v 5.1

a cute puppy picture in
stumpwork embroidery
--v 5.1

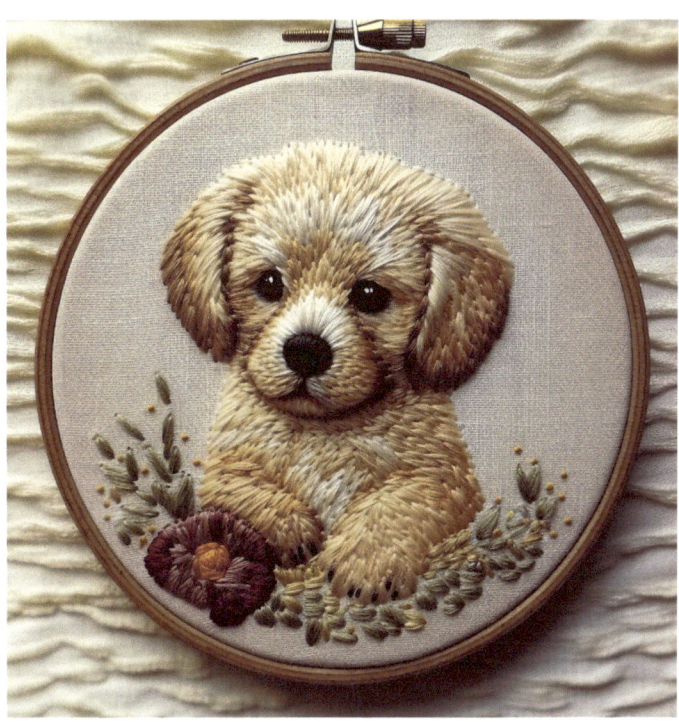

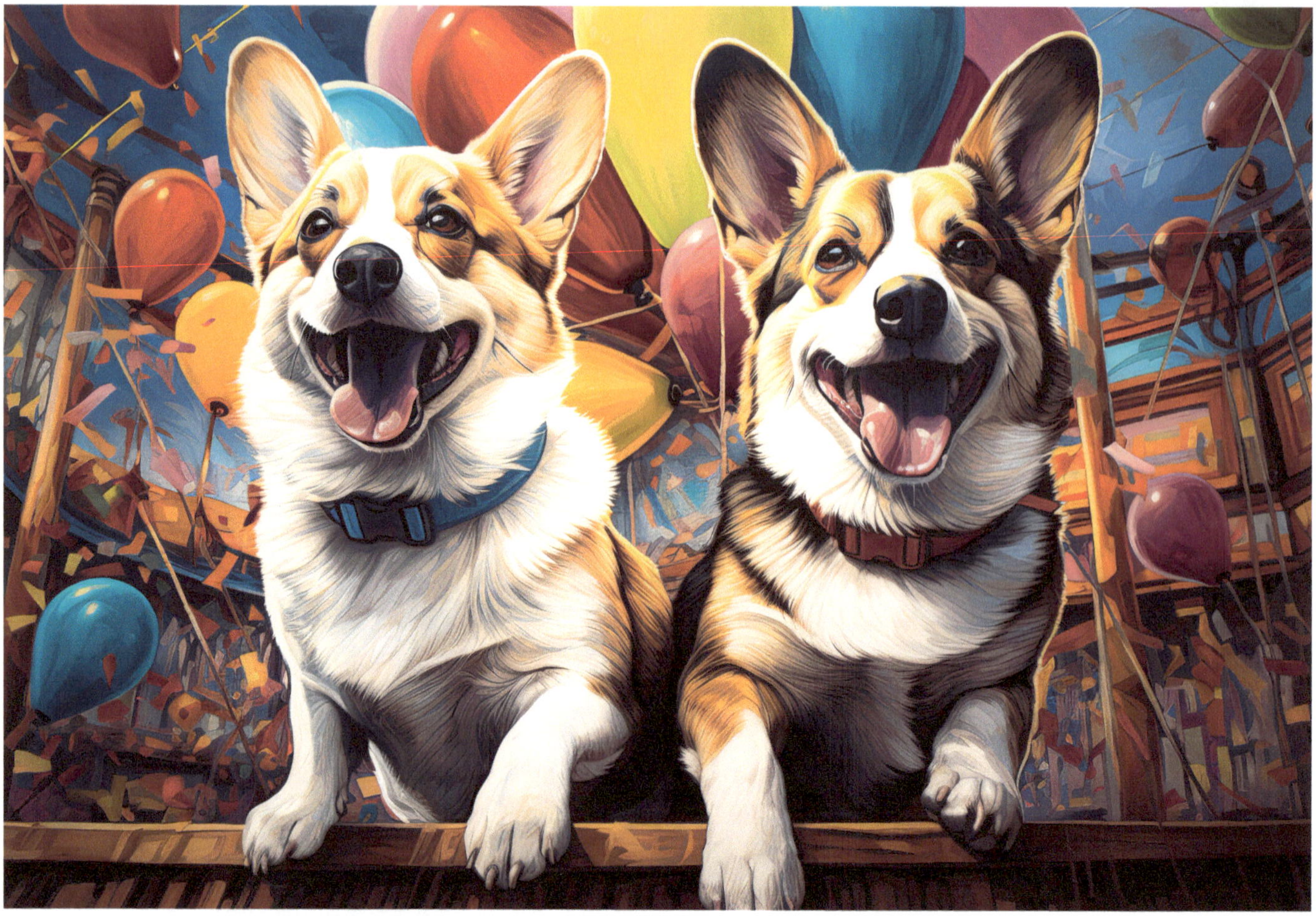

a playful scene in color pencil of Welsh Corgis, short legs and upright ears, racing and playing amidst a colorful carnival backdrop, complete with balloons and a merry-go-round --v 5.2 --ar 3:2

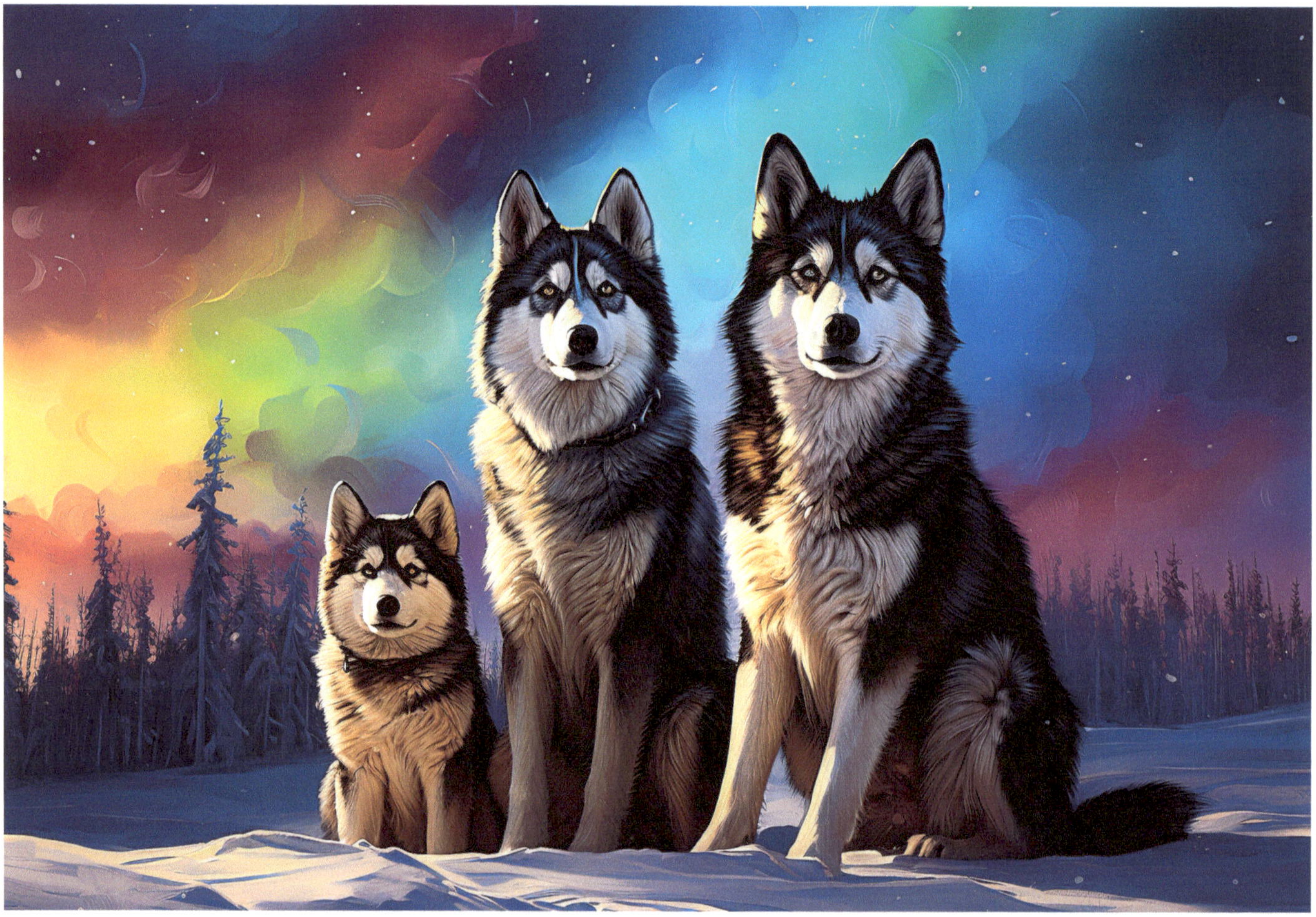

oil painting in the style of Modigliani of Siberian Huskies resting in a snow-covered landscape, with Northern Lights dancing in the sky overhead --v 5.2 --ar 3:2

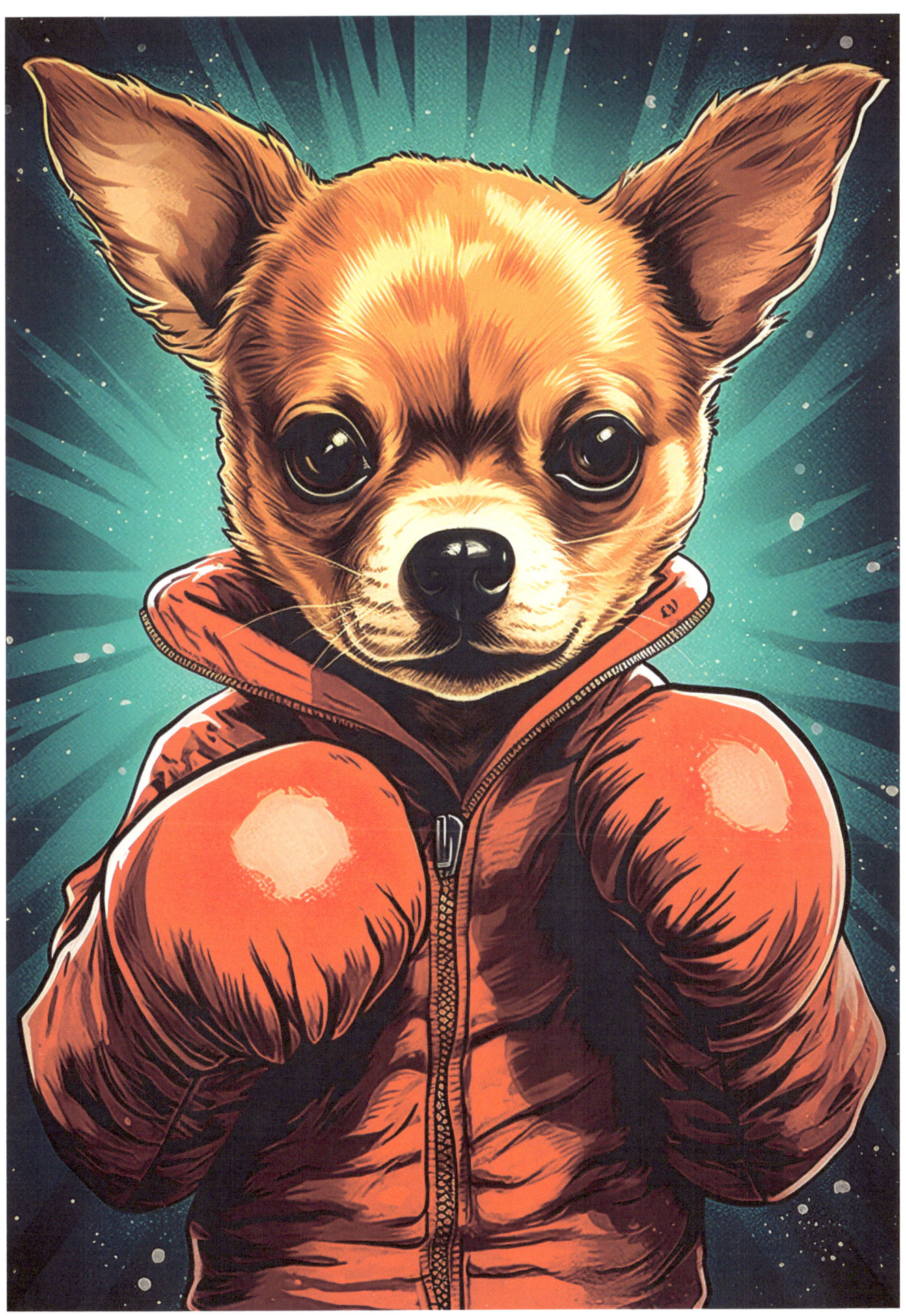

chihuahua dog wears boxing gloves in the style of dan mumford, celebrity portraits, uhd image, decorative paintings, masterful shading, mao hamaguchi --v 5.1 --ar 23:32

Here is some basic helpful information taken from midjourney.com

PROMPTS

A Prompt is a short text phrase that the Midjourney Bot interprets to produce an image. The Midjourney Bot breaks down the words and phrases in a prompt into smaller pieces, called tokens, that can be compared to its training data and then used to generate an image. A well-crafted prompt can help make unique and exciting images.

A basic prompt can be as simple as a single word, phrase or emoji:
/imagine prompt: a cute dog

Prompting Tip!
The Midjourney Bot works best with simple, short sentences that describe what you want to see. Avoid long lists of requests. Instead of: Show me a picture of lots of blooming California poppies, make them bright, vibrant orange, and draw them in an illustrated style with colored pencils Try: Bright orange California poppies drawn with colored pencils

Prompting Notes
Prompt Length
Prompts can be very simple. Single words (or even an emoji!) will produce an image. Very short prompts will rely heavily on Midjourney's default style, so a more descriptive prompt is better for a unique look. However, super-long prompts aren't always better. Concentrate on the main concepts you want to create.

Grammar
The Midjourney Bot does not understand grammar, sentence structure, or words like humans. Word choice also matters. More specific synonyms work better in many circumstances. Instead of big, try gigantic, enormous, or immense. Remove words when possible. Fewer words mean each word has a more powerful influence. Use commas, brackets, and hyphens to help organize your thoughts, but know the Midjourney Bot will not reliably interpret them. The Midjourney Bot does not consider capitalization.

Midjourney Model Version 4 is slightly better than other models at interpreting traditional sentence structure.

Focus on What you Want
It is better to describe what you want instead of what you don't want. If you ask for a party with "no cake," your image will probably include a cake. If you want to ensure an object is not in the final image, try advance prompting using the --no parameter.

Think About What Details Matter
Anything left unsaid may surprise you. Be as specific or vague as you want, but anything you leave out will be randomized. Being vague is a great way to get variety, but you may not get the specific details you want.

Try to be clear about any context or details that are important to you. Think about:

Subject: person, animal, character, location, object, etc.
Medium: photo, painting, illustration, sculpture, doodle, tapestry, etc.
Environment: indoors, outdoors, on the moon, in Narnia, underwater, the Emerald City, etc.
Lighting: soft, ambient, overcast, neon, studio lights, etc
Color: vibrant, muted, bright, monochromatic, colorful, black and white, pastel, etc.
Mood: Sedate, calm, raucous, energetic, etc.
Composition: Portrait, headshot, closeup, birds-eye view, etc.

Use Collective Nouns
Plural words leave a lot to chance. Try specific numbers. "Three cats" is more specific than "cats." Collective nouns also work, "flock of birds" instead of "birds."

Version

Midjourney routinely releases new model versions to improve efficiency, coherency, and quality. The latest model is the default, but other models can be used by adding the --version or --v parameter or by using the /settings command and selecting a model version. Each model excels at producing different types of images.
--version accepts the values 1, 2, 3, 4, 5, 5.1, and 5.2
--version can be abbreviated --v
--v 5.2 is the current default model.

Model Version 5.2
The Midjourney V5.2 model is the newest and most advanced, released June 2023. To use this model, add the --v 5.2 parameter to the end of a prompt, or use the /settings command and select 5 MJ Version 5.2

Default Model 06/22/23–current

This model produces more detailed, sharper results with better colors, contrast, and compositions. It also has a slightly better understanding of prompts than earlier models and is more responsive to the full range of the --stylize parameter.

Model Version 5.1
The Midjourney V5.1 was released on May 4th, 2023. To use this model, add the --v 5.1 parameter to the end of a prompt, or use the /settings command and select 5 MJ Version 5.1

Default Model 05/03/23–06/22/23

This model has a stronger default aesthetic than earlier versions, making it easier to use with simple text prompts. It also has high Coherency, excels at accurately interpreting natural language prompts, produces fewer unwanted artifacts and borders, has increased image sharpness, and supports advanced features like repeating patterns with --tile.

Model Version 5.0
The Midjourney V5.0 model produces more photographic generations than the V5.1 model. This model produces images that closely match the prompt but may require longer prompts to achieve your desired aesthetic.

Default Model 03/30/23–05/03/23

To use this model, add the --v 5 parameter to the end of a prompt, or use the /settings command and select 5 MJ Version 5

Niji Model 5
The Niji model is a collaboration between Midjourney and Spellbrush tuned to produce anime and illustrative styles with vastly more knowledge of anime, anime styles, and anime aesthetics. It's excellent at dynamic and action shots and character-focused compositions.

To use this model, add the --niji 5 parameter to the end of a prompt, or use the /settings command and select 🍏 Niji version 5

This model is sensitive to the --stylize parameter. Experiment with different stylization ranges to fine-tune your images.

Niji Style Parameters
Niji Model Version 5 can also be fine-tuned with --style parameters to achieve unique looks. Try --style cute, --style scenic, --style original (uses the original Niji Model Version 5, which was the default before May 26th, 2023), or --style expressive.

100 artists who have had a significant impact on the history of art and have gained wide recognition.

Leonardo da Vinci	Willem de Kooning	David Hockney
Michelangelo Buonarroti	Jan van Eyck	Yves Klein
Vincent van Gogh	Botticelli	Alexander Calder
Pablo Picasso	Katsushika Hokusai	Ellsworth Kelly
Rembrandt van Rijn	Egon Schiele	Bridget Riley
Claude Monet	Donatello	Frank Stella
Jackson Pollock	Francis Bacon	Toulouse-Lautrec
Salvador Dalí	Yoko Ono	Grant Wood
Frida Kahlo	Auguste Rodin	Jasper Johns
Wassily Kandinsky	Banksy	Gerhard Richter
Caravaggio	Mary Cassatt	Edward Weston
Johannes Vermeer	Kazimir Malevich	Richard Diebenkorn
Francisco Goya	Cy Twombly	Anish Kapoor
Georgia O'Keeffe	Cindy Sherman	Robert Motherwell
Henri Matisse	Edward Hopper	Mark Rothko
Raphael	Ai Weiwei	Brice Marden
Andy Warhol	Damien Hirst	Amedeo Modigliani
Hieronymus Bosch	Joseph Beuys	Frida Kahlo
Albrecht Dürer	Chuck Close	Georges Braque
Titian	Roy Lichtenstein	Constantin Brâncuși
Paul Cézanne	Sandro Botticelli	Agnes Martin
Henri Cartier-Bresson	Lucian Freud	Edward Burne-Jones
Diego Velázquez	Jacob Lawrence	Camille Claudel
Marc Chagall	Tracey Emin	Antonio Canova
Gustav Klimt	James Whistler	Jeff Koons
Jean-Michel Basquiat	Thomas Gainsborough	William Blake
Peter Paul Rubens	William Turner	Betye Saar
Edvard Munch	Anselm Kiefer	Barbara Hepworth
René Magritte	Louise Bourgeois	Nam June Paik
Joan Miró	Keith Haring	Jean Dubuffet
Édouard Manet	Robert Rauschenberg	Sam Gilliam
Artemisia Gentileschi	Norman Rockwell	Louise Nevelson
Pieter Bruegel the Elder	Marcel Duchamp	Romare Bearden
Paul Gauguin		

Note: Some of these artists belong to the more contemporary spectrum, and their significance is still being debated. The list is also biased towards Western artists, though I tried to include artists from a global perspective.

100 Art Styles to experiment with.

Abstract
Academic
Art Deco
Art Nouveau
Baroque
Bauhaus
Byzantine
Classicism
Conceptual
Constructivism
Cubism
Dada
De Stijl
Digital Art
Egyptian
Expressionism
Fauvism
Futurism
Gothic
Graffiti
Greek Classic
Harlem Renaissance
Hudson River School
Impressionism
Installation Art
Kinetic Art
Land Art
Mannerism
Minimalism
Modernism
Neoclassicism
Neo-Expressionism
Neo-Impressionism
Neorealism

Op Art
Orientalism
Outsider Art
Performance Art
Photorealism
Pointillism
Pop Art
Post-Impressionism
Post-Modernism
Precisionism
Pre-Raphaelite
Realism
Renaissance
Rococo
Romanesque
Romanticism
Surrealism
Symbolism
Tonalism
Ukiyo-e
Video Art
Abstract Expressionism
Art Brut
Ashcan School
Color Field Painting
Contemporary
Fantastic Realism
Fluxus
Folk Art
Geometric Abstraction
Hard-edge Painting
Illustration
Japonisme

Magic Realism
Metaphysical Painting
Naïve Art
Naturalism
Northwest School
Orientalist
Photomontage
Plein Air
Post-Painterly Abstract
Primitivism
Regionalism
Russian Avant-Garde
Social Realism
Sound Art
Street Art
Suprematism
Symbolist
Tachisme
Trompe-l'œil
Vorticism
Young British Artists
Arte Povera
COBRA
Gutai
Vienna Secession
Action Painting
Light and Space
Northern Renaissance
New Objectivity
New Media Art
Visionary Art
Indian Miniature
Collage

Remember, the art world is vast, and there are many more styles, movements, and schools of thought than can fit in any list. This selection aims to offer a broad perspective, but it's not exhaustive.

MY LOVELY PETS

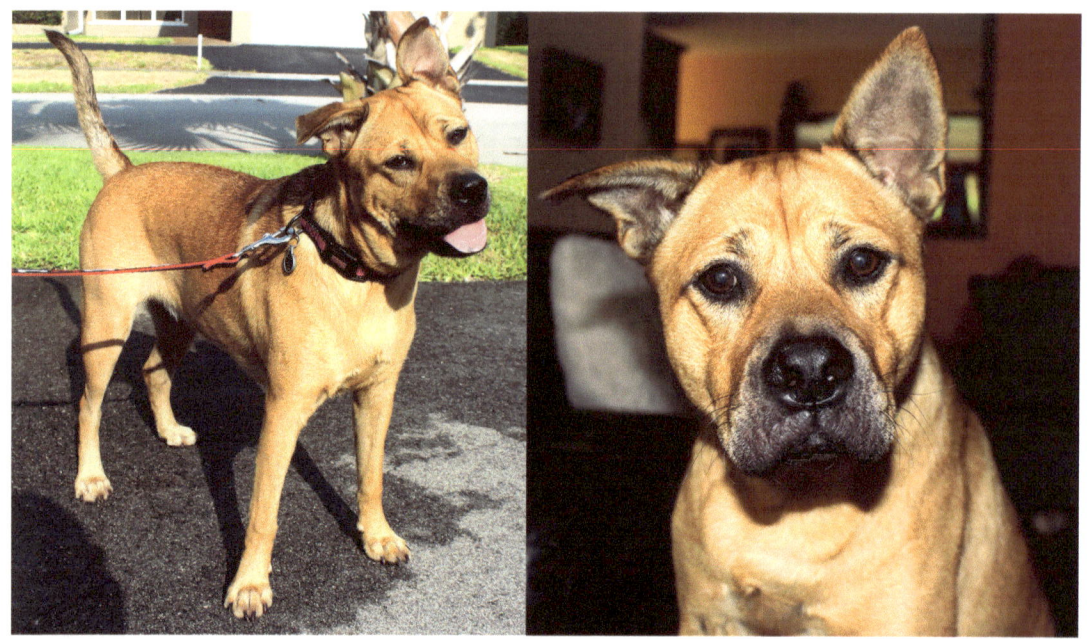

LULU

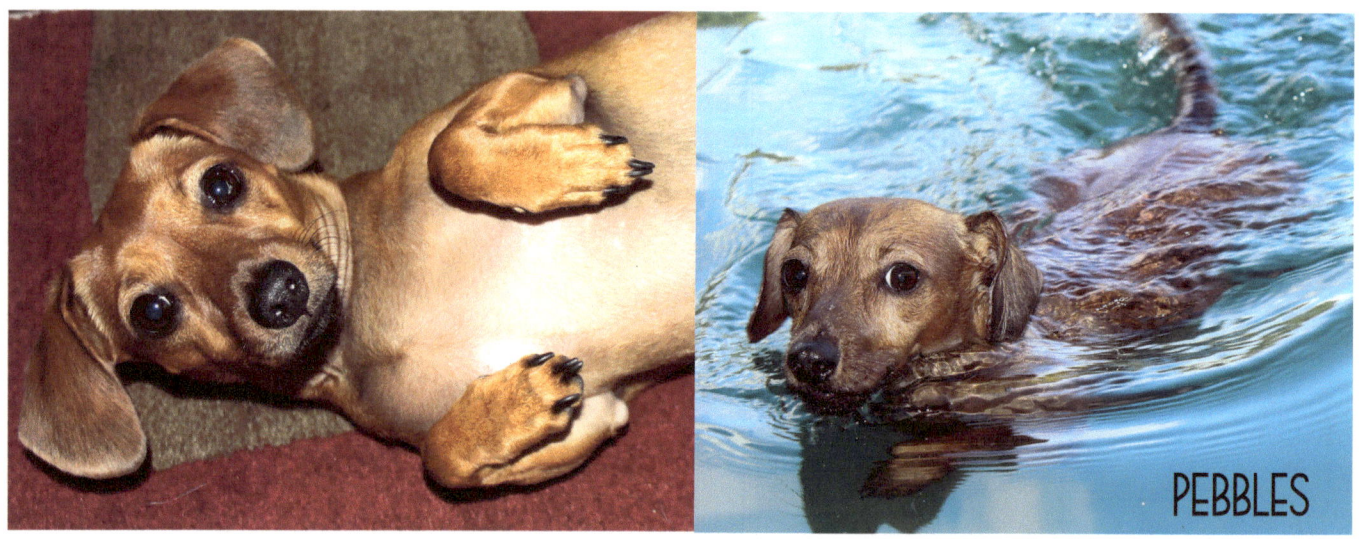

PEBBLES

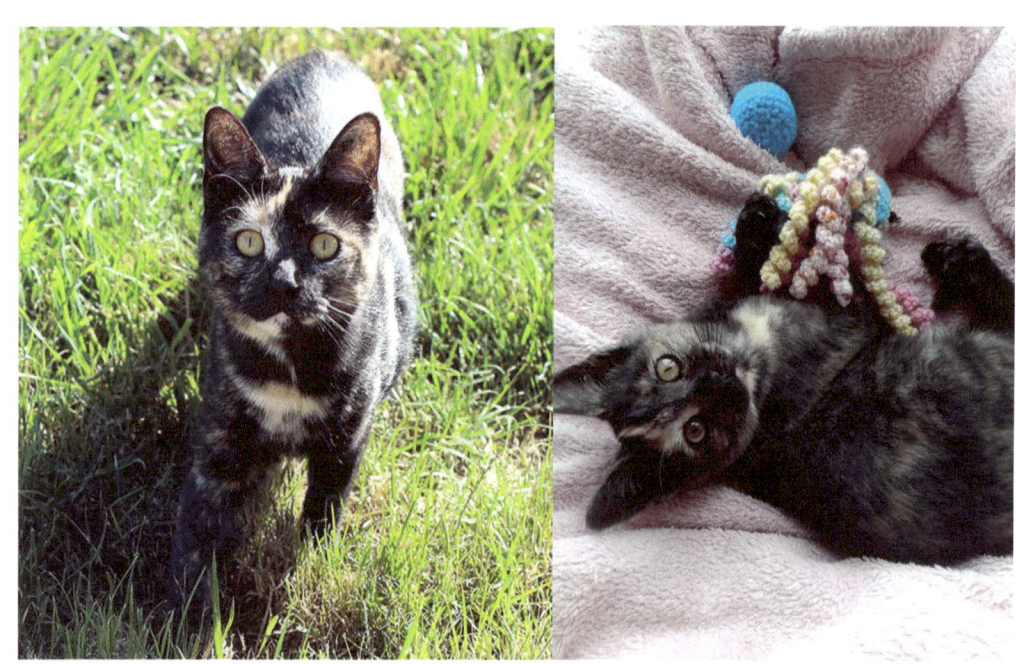

TWIGLET

I hope you have found this book useful and informative as well as enjoyable to look at. I wish you many hours of fun experimenting with these prompts and all the amazing things you can create with A.I. and in particular, the incredible Midjourney application.

Sam Snow

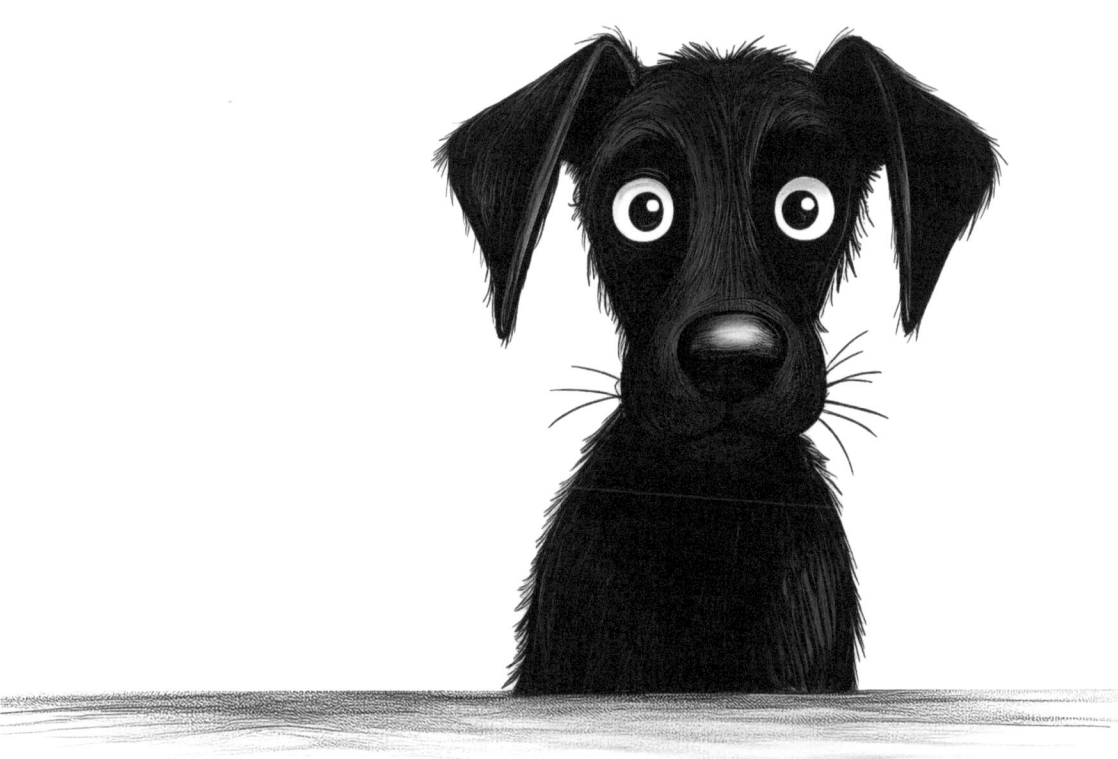

black dog isolated on white background, in the style of jean jullien, hinchel or --v 5.2 --ar 127:99

Cover image prompt:

a dog wearing a hat and tie, in the style of textural prints, red and blue, portraitures, dotted, quadratura, pop culture mash-up, characterful animal portraits --v 5.2 --ar 4:5

www.ingramcontent.com/pod-product-compliance
Lightning Source LLC
Chambersburg PA
CBHW041513280526
45792CB00004B/1240